HOLLYWOOD ON MAIN STREET

BAD AXE (frontispiece)
Watercolor on paper, 1985
12 x 16 in. (30.5 x 40.6 cm.)
Collection: Michael F. Rakosi, New York, N. Y.

HOLLYWOOD oN MAIN STREET

THE MOVIE HOUSE PAINTINGS oF DAVIS CONE

by Linda Chase

THE OVERLOOK PRESS
Woodstock, New York

First published in 1988 by

The Overlook Press
Lewis Hollow Road
Woodstock, New York 12498

Library of Congress Cataloging-in-Publication Data

Chase, Linda
  Hollywood on main street.

    "The movie house paintings of Davis Cone"
    1. Cone, Davis, 1950–   —Themes, motives.
2. Motion picture theaters in art.   3. Photo-realism—
United States.   4. Painting, American.   5. Painting,
Modern—20th century—United States.   I. Cone, Davis,
1950–   . II. Title
ND237.C675C47   1988   759.13   88-5365
ISBN 0-87951-321-7

Book Design by Tenth Avenue Editions

Printed in Hong Kong by South China Printing Company

For my mother, Helen Chase, who loved the movies,
and for the Midway, the Elmwood,
and especially the Trylon,
where my own magical
movie-house memories were born

Acknowledgments

Davis Cone and Linda Chase would like to thank the
following people for their help in the preparation of this
book: Ivan Karp and the staff of the O.K. Harris Gallery,
Michael Rakosi, Charles Moss, Richard Wolfe, William T.
Benedict and the Theatre Historical Society of America.

Davis Cone would particularly like to thank his wife Kathy
for her support and encouragement of his artistic
endeavors and for sharing his love of these old theatres.

Photo credits:

D. James Dee
John Abbott
Lazenby Professional Services, Inc.
New Orleans Museum of Art

CONTENTS

LIST OF PAINTINGS

THE ARTIST AND HIS SUBJECT

COLONIA WITH BOY ON RAIL
Watercolor on paper, 1986
13 x 16 in. (33 x 40.6 cm.)
Collection: High Museum of Art, Atlanta, Ga.

WHEN the small-town movie house closes at the end of Peter Bogdanovich's film *The Last Picture Show*, it marks the passing of innocence for a particular group of high school seniors and becomes a metaphor for the experience of the country as a whole. The time of simple, hometown pleasures is passing for all of us, and in life as in this brilliantly evocative movie, the closing of the neighborhood picture house is one of the most telling signs.

Davis Cone is an artist who has embraced for his subject matter those very small-town theatres—the theatres of his youth—and his concern is not only with the structures themselves and the opportunity they afford to create visually interesting and exciting paintings but with everything they represent. Like the marquees that loom out over the quiet streets of his paintings, these theatres loom large in our collective consciousness. Indeed, no other aspect of twentieth-century American architecture is quite as potent in its ability to elicit nostalgic feeling as the movie houses of our Main Streets. Certainly, part of this attachment is the lost innocence they seem to represent.

For Cone, this attachment is particularly intense. Over the last ten years it has led him to create a remarkable body of work based on the photographs he has taken of the movie houses in and around his native Augusta, Georgia, and on his searches to other locations throughout the country. Working within the Photo Realist tradition, he uses his photographs as source material from which to create highly realistic, meticulously detailed, intensely factual, but also highly evocative "portraits" of the theatres and the small-town streets they inhabit.

The theatre's location is as important for Cone as the theatre itself because it is the contrast between those marvelously gaudy and sometimes even outlandish marquees, with their neon swirls, flashing bulbs, and tracer lights, and the staid and often dowdy streets they inhabit that gives the small-town theatre its special aura. These theatres, built primarily during the golden age of movies from the twenties through the forties, brought a little bit of Hollywood to Main Street, U.S.A.—the Hollywood of glamour and movie stars and happy endings. They seem to promise a special magic and speak to us of a simpler, more optimistic time when a little glitter, a little fantasy sufficed. Cone has a particular fondness for the deco-style neighborhood theatres that sprouted in the 1930s and which most embody that combination of Hollywood glamour and small-town ambience that is at the heart of his interest.

In spite of the objective style of painting Davis Cone employs, his relationship to his subject matter and to the very act of being an artist itself is highly charged with emotion. The theatre paintings both evolve out of and are an expression of attitudes and experiences reaching back to childhood, and this connection to early experiences helps to infuse the paintings with a wonderful sense of magic. They glow not just with the reflected light of brightly lit marquees but with an inner light comprised of artistic inspiration and deep affection.

The artist's own descriptions of his childhood memories are eloquent on the subject of these connections:

"For the two and a half months each painting requires, I am absorbed in a totally different environment and atmosphere. My studio becomes a time machine in which I'm transported very much the way an audience is transported in a movie theatre. Both the painting and the theatre experiences reach back to childhood—to "time out" periods in life. Vacation times.

"My earliest dabblings in paint are associated with the summers I spent with my grandparents in Connecticut. Both were artists and my grandfather, Royal Farnum, was also a professor at and later president of the Rhode Island School of Design. The walls of their pre-Revolutionary War colonial farmhouse were adorned with their own paintings and with the work of their colleagues and of my grandfather's students.

Most of these paintings were from the early 1900s and were typically Impressionistic in style.

"I remember wandering through their cool, dark, low-ceilinged home as a young boy, studying the paintings, absorbed in the magical techniques that transformed paint into trees, pastures, blue skies, and billowing clouds. My grandparents would give me informal art lessons at my request, and then I would choose a location near the house and, with canvas board in lap, I would dip my brush into the paint and try to evoke some of that magic myself. These were wonderful days and wonderful summers—careless and free.

"As for the theatre experiences, they started early too. They were time-outs also—the mini-vacations that came at the end of each week.

"As a child growing up in the nineteen-fifties, I remember the magic of Saturday mornings. Bouncing out of bed early and rushing outside, I would meet my friend Larry and we would pedal our Raleigh bikes down to Thurmond's corner store. Thurmond's was the neighborhood grocer to Mom, but to us it was a wonderland of bubble gum, baseball cards, "red hots," and cold sodas.

"The Saturday morning trip to Thurmond's had a special purpose. As soon as we got there, we would head for the "drink box," the large metal cooler where the cold sodas were kept, dig our hands deep into the slot on the side where the caps fell when the bottles were opened, and fish out six red, blue, and silver Pepsi-Cola tops each.

"Those tops were our movie tickets for the ten a.m. first show at the Imperial Theatre in downtown Augusta. It was a promotional gimmick for Pepsi that Larry and I sidestepped. I'm sure our way of gaining admission was not what some ad man had in mind when he thought it up to increase Pepsi sales, but God bless the "Pepsi Buddy Club" for a lot of great adventures—Tarzan in Africa, Zorro in Mexico, and Flash Gordon out in the galaxies. From my front-row seat life became magnified hundreds of times—my heroes, thirty feet

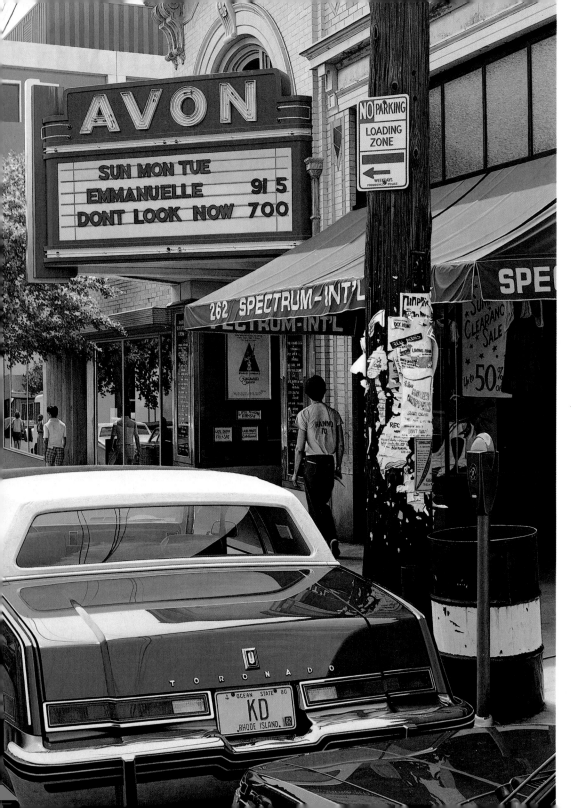

AVON
Acrylic on canvas, 1982
60 x 41½ in. (152.4 x 105.4 cm.)
Private Collection, England

LANE (opposite)
Watercolor on paper, 1986
14 x 15 in. (35.6 x 38.1 cm.)
Collection: Brown & Wood, New York, N. Y.

tall, blazed across a seventy-foot screen.

"Theatres and movies were still major events in those days. Television was just beginning to make its way into American homes and for many of us the theatre was still the place to "see" the news. Newsreels encapsulated with dizzying speed the week's events. Despite the fact that they haven't played in theatres for twenty-five years, I can still hear with crystal clarity the voice of the announcer—a voice of fatherly authority superimposed over the music of a stirring marching band and always seeming to be on the brink of hysteria. It was drama at its best and worst simultaneously. *Here's what's happening in the real world, but settle back— a cartoon and a great escape are about to follow.* That seemed to be the real message.

"In the hushed darkness of the theatre my childhood world expanded. The Saturday morning movies were springboards for the neighborhood gang's activities over the weekend. After the movie, out into the glaring mid-day sun, a couple of ten-cent "Snappy" burgers from next door, and then home to replay our heroes' adventures in our own backyards. Our nineteen-fifties suburb became the dusty plains of the wild West, or the wide, slow-moving Mississippi River, or the steamy jungles of Africa. The downtown theatre was my time machine producing cherished memories for a young daydreamer.

"As I got older it became clear that you never outgrew your local theatre, it just grew up with you. Saturday-morning fantasies were replaced by Friday- and Saturday-night fantasies of another kind, and the prime seat in the house was now in the balcony rather than the front row. The theatre became the romance parlor. Perfume mingled with the smell of hot popcorn, aromas forever associated with the exhilarating freedom of the plush darkness in which the sounds and images flickering on the screen blessedly obscured our adolescent awkwardness. Double dates, blind dates, going steady, breaking up! I can't pass by an old downtown theatre without having flashbacks that run the scope of these emotions.

"I hope my paintings reflect this love I have for the theatres and that they can reawaken, for an instant, personal memories for the viewer as well. It's only one of the levels I hope the viewer will meet my paintings on, but it is an important one for me—that nonartistic gut reaction, like hearing an old song after twenty years and having your mind carried fondly back to the past."

The realist painter is, inevitably, a documentor of his age. In depicting the world around him, he reveals it in new ways for his own time and preserves it for future generations. A tour through the halls of our great museums is a tour not only through art history but also through social and cultural history, and often the things the artist took most for granted in his own day are those which seem the most exotic or revealing to the generations that follow. Vermeer's lush, ordered seventeenth-century Dutch interiors, Monet's Paris railway stations bustling with the energy of the Industrial Revolution, and Edward Hopper's stark, vivid landscapes and streetscapes of Depression-era America, all recall an intensely specific place and time. But often this documentary role is only a byproduct, the natural result of the passing of time and the changes that occur in the world around us.

For Davis Cone the role of chronicler is one he embraces deliberately and wholeheartedly partly because the aspect of the modern world he has chosen to portray is on the verge of disappearing. The invention of television and all its current improvements and accouterments—video cassette recorder, cable, large screen—combined with the suburbanization of the population and the increased reliance on the automobile have taken a severe toll on movie attendance and on the downtown movie house in particular.

The theatres Cone renders so beautifully are an endangered species, rapidly being replaced by the shopping malls' impersonal multiplex cinemas. His work is infused with an almost bardic desire to chronicle this passing age. In fact, it could be said that it is this passing era that is the real subject matter of his work.

Over half the theatres Cone has painted have since closed or been demolished. The evidence of their decline is everywhere in the paintings: marquees sag, neon tubes are broken, exterior tiles are missing, paint is peeling. Some are already defunct, their marquees empty. Others are reduced to showing an X-rated and sensationalist fare that contrasts sadly with the charming grandiloquence of their architecture and often with the dignity and naïveté of their small-town surroundings as well. The theatre in IMPERIAL (p. 19), situated among the dignified, neo-classical structures of Augusta, with its stately trees casting their leafy shadows on the pavement, is showing as a double feature *Devil Dragons* and *Women Never Die.* Other theatres feature *Kung Fu Master,* Adult Entertainment Rated Triple X, and *Emmanuelle.*

These images have tremendous poignancy, made all the more powerful by the artist's dispassionate rendering. In true Photo Realist style, Cone presents the scene factually, letting the subject matter speak for itself. There is no attempt to influence the viewer's response by playing up any of the ironies or anomalies these scenes may contain, or to alter the "found" situations in order to enhance the feelings they evoke. Nevertheless, the artist's involvement is everywhere apparent.

Factual as a Photo Realist painting might be, it *is* a painting, and every step of the artist's input is crucial to its effect. From the moment Davis Cone decides to photograph a particular theatre in order to paint it, through all the decisions necessary to take the photographs, choose the composition, and orchestrate the myriad decisions that go into the painting process itself, the artist leaves his stamp. For it is one of the ironies of Photo Realism that no matter how objective the artist may try to be through his use of a photographic source and reliance on the "found" situation he chooses to paint,

IMPERIAL
Acrylic on canvas, 1977
34 x 48 in. (86.4 x 121.9 cm.)
Collection: E. Gordon Stringer, Atlanta, Ga.

the painting itself can never be objective. The result may be an image that stuns us with its factual veracity and verisimilitude, but long after the initial thrill of recognition, it continues to intrigue us and to hold our attention as a work of art precisely because it has been informed and enlivened by the artist's personal vision.

CINEMA (work in progress, detail)

PAL (detail, opposite)

VARIETY PHOTOPLAYS
Acrylic on canvas, 1983
50½ x 37½ in. (128.3 x 95.2 cm.)
Collection: Michael F. Rakosi, New York, N. Y.

EVERETT (opposite)
Watercolor on paper, 1987
12 x 17½ in. (30.5 x 44.5 cm.)
Collection: The Artist

THE LOEW'S GRAND:

FROM OPERA HOUSE

TO MOVIE HOUSE

WHEN the Loew's Grand opened in Atlanta, Georgia, in 1893, it wasn't the Loew's, it wasn't the Grand, it wasn't even a movie theatre, and it didn't look anything like it did when Davis Cone began painting it in 1976.

The Loew's was the first theatre Cone painted, and it is interesting both for its place in the history of his work and for the history of the theatre itself. Like so many theatres that were to become the movie houses of the future, the Loew's began its existence as a legitimate theatre, opening in 1893 as De Give's Grand Opera House, a dramatic center dedicated to the live presentation of opera, Shakespeare, and melodrama.

The opening of the theatre was an august occasion treated with suitable fanfare. It was the third largest structure of its kind in the United States at the time, and was unique for being a combined office building and theatre, and also for having an atrium in the center of the building. But to those who attended opening night, the electric chandeliers, personally designed by Laurent De Give, were probably the most astonishing aspect. Electricity was still a novelty at the time and the *Atlanta Constitution* proclaimed the Grand's "incandescents" a "revelation," suggesting that such lights might someday be adopted to good effect in private homes.

By 1916 the economic advantages of multiple theatre ownership were already becoming apparent and theatre impresarios like Marcus Loew were busy expanding their holdings. The Grand was acquired by the Loews Theatre chain that year, and like many of the picture palaces of the time, began showing combined programs of vaudeville and silent films. But the Grand was to undergo an even greater transformation in 1932 when the old theatre was gutted and transformed in the new art deco style by the renowned theatre architect Charles Lamb.

Lamb, along with John Eberson and the Rapp brothers, had made his reputation designing the large, elaborate, fantasy-laden "picture palaces" of the late teens and twenties,

LOEW'S: ATLANTA
Acrylic on canvas, 1976-77
36 x 24 in. (91.4 x 61 cm.)
Private Collection, Augusta, Ga.

MARTIN (opposite)
Acrylic on canvas, 1980
35½ x 47½ in. (90.2 x 120.7 cm.)
Collection: Barbara and Richard Lane, New York, N. Y.

beginning with a dignified if ornate Adam style, and running through the wildly eclectic French baroque and Oriental-Hindu themes that were to turn movie houses into Xanadus of entertainment. As Marcus Loew's favorite of the theatre architects, Lamb was called upon to design the majority of the theatres in the Loews chain, an empire that would eventually cover half the country.

By 1932, the new "Moderne" style (as it was then called), which had its beginnings in the *Exposition des Arts Décoratifs et Industriels Modernes* in Paris in 1925, had been quickly embraced by Hollywood and was de rigueur. The Grand was completely gutted and rebuilt in this new style, and while most of the more elaborate art deco embellishments were reserved for the inside, the front did gain a new V-shaped marquee edged in aluminum, an enormous "Loew's" written in script perched rakishly on top, and beveled aluminum curves on either side of the entrance.

From its beginnings as an opera house through its transformation to a movie theatre, the Grand had always been one of the showplaces of the South, but its position in theatre history and in the hearts of Southerners was assured on December 15, 1939, when it hosted the premiere of the greatest soap opera of all time, the four-hour Civil War epic *Gone With the Wind*. It was a premiere on the grandest scale, with the governors of eight Southern states in attendance, as well as the stars of the film—Vivien Leigh, Clark Gable, and Olivia de Havilland—and a veritable "Who's Who" of notables including J.P. Morgan, John Jacob Astor, and Nelson Rockefeller.

The deco façade of the theatre was hidden for the occasion behind a columned portico built to resemble Scarlett O'Hara's plantation house, Tara, while the local population decked itself out in hoop skirts, Rhett Butler mustaches, and other antebellum finery.

After this glorious occasion, the history of the theatre was rather humdrum (except for the second world premiere of *Gone With the Wind* when the film was re-released), operating as just another Loews downtown theatre through the sixties and early seventies, outlasting three other Atlanta picture palaces, the Paramount, the Rialto, and the Roxy, partly by turning to a black-oriented film program.

Architecturally the theatre remained essentially the same for nearly four decades while the office towers of modern Atlanta rose around it. The result is a disconcerting contrast which is artfully employed in Davis Cone's painting, LOEW'S: ATLANTA (p. 27). The marquee looms out over the narrow street, asserting itself against the surrounding buildings, which seem to threaten suffocation with their proximity. The denseness of the composition accentuates this "war" between the two elements which, at least in the context of the painting, seems to result in a draw. The marquee retains its Hollywood flamboyance, hinting at former glory, but the titles of the exploitation films it advertises, *Curse the Devil* and *Scream Bloody Murder,* tell another story, blasting the appeal of murder and mayhem in opposition both to the antiseptic blandness of the other structures in the painting and to the theatre's history. Implicit in the painting is a double message—not only is this a theatre about to be swallowed by a hostile environment, but the world that spawned it is threatened as well.

"I sell tickets to theatres, not movies," Marcus Loew is famous for asserting, displaying both his pride in his theatre chain and his conviction that a great theatre drew patrons regardless of what was shown. But that was before the advent of television and suburban culture and shopping malls, and before the economics of the multiplex theatre took its toll. In January 1978, a year after Cone painted it, the Loew's Grand burned down just as the Atlanta Urban Design Commission was seeking proposals to save it.

The LOEW'S: ATLANTA was Davis Cone's first theatre painting, but when he painted it he had no idea it would be the start of a series. At that time he was doing paintings

MARIANNE
Acrylic on canvas, 1984
40½ x 59½ in. (102.9 x 151.1 cm.)
Collection: H. Theodore Greene, Calif.

MARTIN: TALLEDEGA (opposite)
Acrylic on canvas, 1981
43 x 40 in. (109.2 x 101.6 cm.)
Collection: Edward J. Minskoff, New York, N. Y.

of urban and suburban imagery in and around the area where he grew up, and his concern in painting this scene was with the urban landscape rather than with the theatre itself. However, while he was painting the Loew's, he continued to photograph material for future paintings and was inspired to photograph another theatre, the Imperial in Augusta, the home of his childhood movie-house adventures. It seemed a natural for his next painting.

"All of the other subject matter I had done seemed a little too banal for me, a little too emotionally detached," he says. "I wanted to paint something I felt an attachment to. I decided to paint my hometown theatre, and when it was finished I looked at the two paintings together. I liked the way they related to each other and decided I wanted to explore this idea further."

Like the Loew's, the Imperial is portrayed at an angle looking down a city street, but here the mood is much more bucolic. The vista opens up to sky as our eye moves past the theatre, traveling with the traffic down Broad Street, which seems to be going at a leisurely Southern pace. Instead of the cold gray metal and glass of Atlanta, the stone and marble buildings of Augusta emit a warm ivory glow, and the potted trees that line the sidewalk soften the scene with their filigreed shadows.

But the Imperial, with its large white neon box letters shadowed in crimson, and its tracer lights outlining the top and bottom of the marquee, is just as out of context in its block of dignified columns and neo-classical structures as the Loew's is in downtown Atlanta. Unfortunately, the sense of dislocation this creates is compounded here as well by the attractions featured on the marquee, *Devil Dragons* and *Women Never Die*. Or is it *Devil Women* and *Dragons Never Die*? It hardly matters; the message comes across loud and clear. The marquees themselves, in their new dowager re-spectability (for it is one of the ironies of these paintings that what was once flashy becomes decorous over time), seem somehow affronted by these indignities, as if they know they were never intended to show such fare.

Although neither of the theatres in these first two paintings is, strictly speaking, a "small-town" theatre (one is situated in a large and the other in a small city), and neither one was actually built in the deco era (the Imperial was built in 1917), two of the major themes of Cone's theatre series have already been delineated—the decline of the downtown movie theatre and the resulting poignant contrast between former glory and current distress, and the architectural dislocation caused by the presence of the marquee itself.

Unlike the builders of the conservative buildings and storefronts on either side of them, theatre owners and designers were under no compunction to fit in or follow local architectural constraints. In fact, the gaudier the better. The essence of these theatres was to be "theatrical"; and from the early days of the nickelodeons through the age of the great picture palaces and on into the era of art deco embellishments, the designers let their imaginations run wild, curbed only by the constraints of budget, which in the smaller theatres was a factor that sometimes came into play, limiting the number and size, if not the spirit, of the adornments.

In their gaudy architecture, the marquees capture, in Cone's words, "the flashy, outlandish, golden years of Hollywood." They captured it and brought it to life in towns all across America, creating an aura of magic—to enter their doors was to be transported to another world.

Cone goes on to describe some of the effects that make his childhood memories of these theatres so compelling: "In contrast to the adjacent brick and wood buildings, the theatres were often covered with high-gloss opaque glass panels (Vitrolite tiles) that reflected the marquee and lights—doubling the maze of visual activity. Add to this—Aztec inlays, chrome clocks, glass block back-lit with neon, porthole windows, Indian headdresses lit up with multicolored neon "feathers," and on and on—and you begin to envision the

RITZ
Acrylic on canvas, 1982
37 x 54 in. (94 x 137.2 cm.)
Private Collection, Tennessee

KNOX
Watercolor on paper, 1985
9 x 15½ in. (22.7 x 39.4 cm.)
Collection: Michael F. Rakosi, New York, N. Y.

wild freedom designers were allowed in those rather ordinary, quiet, conservative towns."

Even the simplest marquee tends to dominate its surroundings. The sheer mass of it jutting out over the sidewalk is an anomaly. When you add to that the lights and lettering, you have a truly overpowering presence. It is not clear exactly when the first flashing, light-studded marquees came into being, but at some point in the early part of the century the plain canopies that were characteristic of the old opera houses and legitimate theatres were married to the sparkle and hoopla achieved around the entrances of the flashier nickelodeons to create a structure that was at once canopy and sign, protection from the weather and beacon to lure the passerby.

"In looking at each theatre," Cone says, "I try to capture its strange interaction with the surroundings. The marquee serves such an unusual architectural function: there's no other building that has this huge protrusion. Other buildings have awnings, but nothing as weighty or as awkwardly heavy as the marquees." Throughout the theatre series, the weight and structure of the marquees is a major compositional element, either dominating the composition and almost engulfing the pictorial space, as in GREENSBORO THEATRE (p. 90), CO- LONIA WITH BOY ON RAIL (p. 10), PARK (p. 54), and MILLER (p. 99), or asserting a disconcerting presence in the middle distance of an ordinary small-town street, as in WILKES (p. 62), WINK (p. 63), MARTIN (p. 26), and MARIANNE (p. 30). But of all the theatres Cone has painted so far, the prize for the most disconcerting, the most whimsical, the most compelling and overwhelming marquee would indisputably have to go to the Roxy.

THE PAINTINGS AND THE THEATRES

A SMALL-TOWN SUCCESS STORY:

THE ROXY

NORTHAMPTON, PA.

All you hear about these days is the ever-lasting cry of theatre managers that they are looking for "what the people want." . . . The people themselves don't know what they want. They want to be entertained, that's all. Don't "give the people what they want"—give 'em something better.

S. L. (Roxy) Rothapfel
Green Book Magazine, 1914

Northampton, Pennsylvania, population 8,200, is a town that has seen better days. The rows of low brick facades that line the main street show jarring gaps where buildings have been torn down, and many of the storefronts that remain are vacant. The plate glass and aluminum façade of the new discount drug store looks at once too modern and lively for the tired respectability of the rest of the town and too brash and tacky—an affront—a piece of the mall dropped down out of context. The empty streets give very little indication of where the customers are supposed to come from, and there don't appear to be any other signs of a renaissance in the making, if that's what the drug store represents.

Northampton is a town by-passed by progress, and therein lies its charm. It exudes an aura of friendly nostalgia, evoking an instant longing for a time when such places with their good hard-working people and honest values were the backbone of America. A time and place that may in fact have existed only in our collective fantasies—and in the movies. For movies, while they are expressions of both our reality and our dreams, often confuse the one with the other.

So it makes sense that except for the drugstore the only sign of vitality on Northampton's drab main street—a sign that this was once a thriving, lively little place after all—is its movie theatre. And what a movie theatre it is! And what a marquee it has! Lit up, in all its glory, as it is in Davis Cone's watercolor, ROXY (p. 38), it flaunts its existence, spewing its light profligately across the street and casting a glow so intense it must be visible for miles. There are so many lights—neon lights, multicolored stud lights—it virtually pulses with electricity. Not an inch remains undecorated or unlit. And the lights don't just sit there, they flash the name "Roxy," first vertically, then horizontally, into the night.

The Roxy is a small theatre, seating only six hundred, but its marquee could clearly hold its own with the most ornate two-thousand-seat picture palace. For the little street on which it sits, the marquee is enormous, the side panels

ROXY
Watercolor on paper, 1987
11½ x 16¾ in. (29.2 x 42.5 cm.)
Collection: Michael F. Rakosi, New York, N. Y.

rising nearly to the rooftops of the two-story buildings that flank it. Everything in Cone's painting conspires to emphasize the charm and overbearing magnitude of this outlandish structure. Captured just before nightfall on a rainy evening, the Roxy's orange and yellow lights cast a lurid glow against the purple sky. The offset arrangement of shadowy cars parked along the darkening street and the light that spills between them from the theatre itself combine to draw our eye to the theatre entrance, while the brilliant white of the stud lights and milk glass advertising panels under the marquee emphasize its depth and prevent it from appearing top-heavy.

As for the style of the marquee—well, it's hard to say. The theatre was remodeled in the 1930s and the vertical panels have a kind of stepped-back deco skyscraper, or Mayan, configuration, but the curling scrolls and feather motif on top counter any hint of streamline. It looks, in fact, a little like a dancer of questionable background decked out in sequins and feathered headdress for the Folies-Bergères. Or perhaps she is sitting bare-legged astride the neck of a circus elephant, leading the parade. Suffice it to say that the marquee of the Roxy gives flamboyance a new name—which wouldn't have bothered the original "Roxy" one bit.

The name, Roxy, connotes that special razzle-dazzle showiness Hollywood is famous for, and with good reason, for it is the name of one of motion pictures' great original showmen. "Roxy" Rothapfel (later changed to Rothafel) was in his time the greatest showman of them all. Roxy's personal history, entertainingly documented in Ben Hall's book *The Best Remaining Seats*, is the history of movie theatres personified. His career began and flowered in the teens and twenties as the movie theatres were beginning and developing, and their fortunes were intertwined.

In 1907, after stints at several unsatisfying careers—including door to door salesman, livery driver, and baseball player for a minor league team in Pennsylvania (where he got his nickname)—Roxy got a job in a tavern in the small Pennsylvania town of Forest City and married the beautiful daughter of the tavern owner. Before too long he convinced his father-in-law to let him open a theatre in a large room behind the bar. This was the perfect place, he figured, to show those "living pictures" that had become so popular in larger towns.

"Rothapfel's Family Theatre," as it was called, opened on New Year's Day 1908, with Roxy himself meeting the train in Carbondale at four-thirty in the morning to pick up the Vitagraph reels, which he had to lug seven miles through the snow back to the theatre. Roxy was the proverbial one-man band; he painted the posters, distributed the handbills, ran the projector, booked the shows, and even explained the action taking place on the screen to the audience. He was constantly thinking up new things to bring people in: a curtain that closed over the screen between reels, lights concealed around the screen that changed from pink to green to blue during the show as he threw the switches, musicians to play classical selections between the films.

With all these innovations, Roxy's reputation spread. People in the city began to hear about his classy little operation and soon he was hired away to improve theatre operations elsewhere. He traveled first to Minneapolis, then to Chicago, and on to Milwaukee, where he helped to turn the fortunes of a large, handsome, but failing vaudeville house by introducing motion pictures—but motion pictures shown with real style and class. Today, we tend to think of the invention of motion pictures as an instant success, but though a novelty, early movies were poorly made and usually poorly shown. Compared to vaudeville and other forms of legitimate theatre, they were considered a lowly form of entertainment.

Roxy's early efforts as an impresario coincided with the maturing of the movies themselves. The first feature films telling complete stories were just beginning to be made. When Roxy finally fulfilled his dream and became the manager of a New York theatre, it was for the Regent on 116th Street and

Seventh Avenue, the first deluxe theatre built in New York specifically for showing movies. Most neighborhood movie houses of the time were throwbacks to the early nickelodeons and the audiences were made up primarily of children and working-class people looking for inexpensive amusement. The real theatre-going public was not ready to accept movies as serious entertainment and the Regent was losing money badly. Roxy came in and worked his magic, turning an evening at the Regent into an event. He understood that to elevate the movies from the taint of their working-class nickelodeon beginnings it was necessary to give them the trappings of the stage, to showcase them in the right environment in combination with other "highbrow" entertainment.

To achieve the proper ambience, he built a setting for the screen representing a conservatory with real plants, an actual electric fountain, and windows through which, at various times, singers could be seen. His most important innovation at the Regent, however, was the music. Although all the large theatres in these days of silent movies had musicians, they played standard selections that had little to do with the film. Roxy brought in and trained a full-scale orchestra that played classical pieces he personally scored to relate to the action and mood on the screen—a revolutionary idea that added immensely to the film-going experience. Although he has been accused of belittling the movies themselves with his staged extravaganzas, Roxy understood their potential and he knew the secret to all magic was to have nothing interfere with its spell.

Not long after his success at the Regent, he became manager of the Strand, another new, ornate theatre on Broadway designed expressly for movies by Charles Lamb. Here he instituted another innovation—the showing of the feature film without breaks. Using four projectors, he was able to show nine reels of fifteen minutes each without having to stop. The audience was mesmerized.

Roxy had made it to Broadway, but he still dreamed of

having his own theatre, one named after him, and on March 11, 1927, Roxy's "Cathedral of the Motion Picture" opened with mind-boggling pomp and ceremony. By that time the scale and ornateness of both the architecture and the presentation had reached a mad crescendo. The Roxy was billed as *the most sumptuous and stupendous theatre ever erected,* with a stated cost of $10,000,000 and an advertised seating capacity of 6200. The premiere attraction on the screen opening night was Gloria Swanson's, *The Love of Sunya,* but that was just a small part of an evening that included performances of a symphonic tone poem on the writing of the "Star Spangled Banner" in which cannons boomed, a full-scale floral fantasy ballet, a choral and dance "Fantasy of the South," and a symphonic "Russian Lullaby," which Irving Berlin was commissioned to write especially for the opening night. All of this was accompanied by spectacular scenic and lighting effects and was capped by a performance of the overture from Bizet's *Carmen* during which a film of the Metropolitan Opera chorus and ballet was projected on a screen behind the live orchestra. In an early instance of sound in movies, the filmed singers were seen and *heard.*

There were also specially filmed greetings from President Coolidge, Mayor Walker of New York, and others, and a clip showing three hundred patients at Walter Reed Hospital arranged on the lawn to spell Roxy's name. It was then announced that the proceeds from the opening night would be used to buy radios for patients in veterans hospitals across the country. Roxy was nothing if not a showman.

The radios had a special significance because, oddly enough, it was radio that had made Roxy truly famous, bringing his voice into homes across America and making his name synonymous with the movies. In 1922 Roxy had made his first broadcast from the Capitol theatre, the largest, grandest theatre he had managed at that time and the center of the Capitol Wheel, Goldwyn Pictures' chain of forty theatres. Doomsayers had been predicting for at least a year that radio

would be the death of the movies. The image of theatre goers staying home, their ears glued to the radio speaker, was an industry nightmare (a nightmare that would later become a reality with another medium, television). But with characteristic optimism, Roxy pooh-poohed the threat and jumped at the chance to do his own broadcasts—if you can't fight 'em, join 'em. No one could have predicted the tremendous hit Roxy would make as he took to the microphone.

His first broadcast, on November 19, 1922, was the regular presentation of the Capitol stage show. From the wings, he described for the listeners the dancers, scenery, and costumes and also mentioned the wonderful movie playing at the Capitol that night. The next day the lines were around the block. Letters poured in to the station praising the music and the man "with the nice friendly voice who told us about the show." The Capitol shows became a regular Sunday evening event, Roxy's warm, friendly voice was broadcast to millions across America—and there was always a subtle plug for the movie currently playing at the Capitol. Roxy, the show, and radio itself became enormously popular, but there was always that reminder "to get out and go to the movies."

So it is no surprise that theatre owners would want to borrow some of Roxy's allure by using his name on their marquees, and it is especially appropriate in the case of the Northampton Roxy, which is situated only sixty or seventy miles from the original "Rothapfel's Family Theatre." And it is also fitting that the current owner of the Northampton Roxy, Richard Wolfe, has saved and revived this marvelous little theatre with some of the same flair for showmanship and understanding of the value and importance of the trappings of the theatrical experience as his theatre's namesake.

To go to the Roxy today is to be transported back to the time when going to the movies was an event. Of course, the experience begins with the marquee, which beckons with its splendor, but the magic doesn't stop there.

The staff—from the the ticket seller to the usher to the person selling popcorn and soft drinks at the concession stand—all wear Roxy uniforms. For the doorman this includes burgundy jacket, gray pants with burgundy stripes down the legs, bow tie, and epaulets. The finishing touch is the official Roxy pin worn on the lapel. The pins bear the new logo of the theatre, the word Roxy in a fan-shaped deco design. (Roxy himself put great store in the appearance and behavior of his ushers, who were trained like West Point cadets to be proud, neat, efficient, polite, and gracious.) Usually Wolfe is there as well, also in uniform, to greet patrons and add that personal touch only a dedicated manager/owner can provide.

After you give your ticket to the uniformed doorman, you go through the lobby with its deco-design sconces and wall motifs and into the auditorium itself, the plush seats and carpeting restored by Wolfe but the walls and ceiling bearing the original deco damask and elaborately painted stylized geometric designs. The original chandeliers, which have been described as "china meets art-deco," glow, and the screen is hidden by a lush curtain. To complete the mood, taped old-time organ music is playing (an original theatre organ has been obtained and is awaiting installation). Before the show begins, the chandeliers are dimmed one color and tier at a time—first amber, then red, then blue—to fifty percent. Then the amber stage lights slowly begin to fade until all that is left are the red footlights and the blue border lights across the top. The music is timed perfectly so that the piece ends as the curtains open with no gap between the organ music and the music from the screen and no overlap, either. The remaining stage lights fade as the curtain parts, again timed perfectly to be completely off when the curtain is open.

What appears then is the newest addition to the show, the Roxy logo, filmed with fanfare to the accompaniment of marvelously dated music, looking and sounding exactly like the old studio logos we all remember from the forties and fifties. It's impossible not to laugh and applaud in recognition

WINK (detail, opposite)

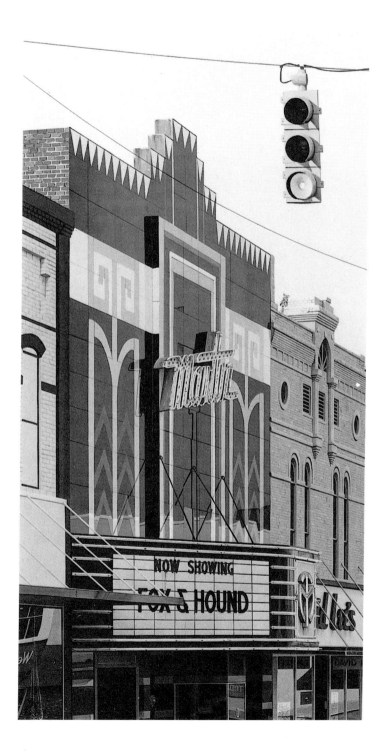

of both the nostalgia and the showmanship. After this comes the cartoon. Yes, cartoon, the old-fashioned "Looney Tunes" and "Merry Melodie" variety, which Wolfe rents from a distributor he has ferreted out. This is followed by the coming attraction (Wolfe believes in showing only one preview). A sign appears briefly on the screen—*Remember, the new show starts Friday*—before the curtain closes again. The red footlights come up and the house lights, which have remained at fifty percent to allow for people who are still coming in, fade away. By the time the curtain reopens, timed, again perfectly, to reveal the studio logo of the main feature, the theatre is dark. Every moment of it—lights fading, changing colors, coming up and going down again in perfect unison with music and curtains—is a pleasure to watch, and it all heightens the sense of glamour and occasion which is the essence of this kind of movie-going experience.

The theatre was originally built in 1921 as the Lyric by Harry Hartman, Northampton's first movie-house entrepreneur. It was advertised originally as having one thousand seats, over four hundred more than it has today. In those days, when bigger was definitely assumed to be better, it was common policy to round off the number to the nearest thousand, and to count every seat in the theatre—including the stools in the box office and the projection room and the couches in the lobby and the lounges.

Hartman built the first nickelodeon in town and then took over the first Lyric Theatre across the street (now a luncheonette). In 1921 he opened the new Lyric as a combined vaudeville and picture house, retaining the old name. At that time film was paid for by a flat rental based on the number of seats you had—if you had more seats they assumed you did more business—and also based upon the glamour of the theatre. If you had a luxurious "palace" you paid more than if you had just a plain nickelodeon or small theatre. The new Lyric was much larger and much more ornate than the original one, but Hartman never told the film distributor, and he went on paying the old, cheap film prices. It wasn't until 1933, when Hartman sold out to Clark and Greenberg Theatres of Philadelphia, that it was renovated in its current deco style and renamed the Roxy.

Decline for the Roxy came with a dramatic decrease in box-office receipts when the Whitehall Mall opened in 1962, introducing the first shopping-center theatre in the area. Clark and Greenberg leased the theatre out to other operators in that year after making some unfortunate "improvements," including resheathing the box office and entry wall in prefabricated wood paneling and painting everything, even the lettering, beige and black. The new managers did nothing to improve matters. By 1970 there was virtually no business at all. Richard Wolfe describes his first experiences at the Roxy:

"I went on a Thursday night and parked across the street. They had only one show on weeknights at seven-thirty, so I was here at ten after seven because I wanted to see them open up. I wanted to see the marquee light up and observe people going in, and so forth. At a quarter after no one was waiting to go in, no lights went on, no one came out to the box office. Finally, a couple of people came up and were standing around waiting. The box office opened up at twenty-five after seven and the only lights they lit up were the three rosettes under the marquee, they never lit up the marquee itself. This was in May and it was still pretty light out so I thought maybe they didn't need it.

"I bought my ticket and went in. The door in the back of the box office was wide open, which I thought was odd for security reasons. There was no doorman taking tickets. There was a very small concession stand and the guy selling the refreshments took the tickets. It was seven-thirty. Time for the show to start, but it didn't start. I counted the people—there were eight of us. Seven-thirty-five rolled by and the man by the concession stand stuck his head around the corner and yelled, 'You can come back out for a refund. There's not enough people, we won't be running the show.' I knew

MARTIN: TALLEDEGA (detail, opposite)

then that if I was nuts enough to take over the theatre I could never do that. You've got to run the show at all costs. You can't chase people away. The picture they were running the night I came to the theatre was, appropriately enough, *Take the Money and Run.*

"In spite of this experience, I came and looked at it again, and it seemed like nothing was going well that time either. The owner showed me the theatre, but he had no idea where the light switches were—or so he said. Maybe he was afraid to turn the lights on. We actually looked at the auditorium with a flashlight. It was in terrible condition. Most of the seats were just springs, some had no backs. Whole rows of seats would just flip over—it was dangerous for someone to come in and sit down. The carpeting in the lobby was worn through to the boards and someone had tacked a runner on top of it which was already threadbare. The auditorium ceiling was totally flaking, paint was hanging down everywhere. The stage curtain was ripped and the curtain motor was gone.

"But I looked at the community, and at that time Northampton was fairly thriving, and I thought, it's just the management, they've let the place go, they didn't know what they were doing. They weren't theatre people (one was a pharmacist and the other an accountant), and they probably thought all they had to do was unlock the doors and people would come rushing in. So I decided I'd take a chance. And I did, but it was downright awful in the beginning."

Wolfe's love of old theatres goes back to his high-school days, when he worked as an usher at the Boyd theater in Easton. The Boyd was a 1800-seat "atmospheric" house. The atmospheric theatre was the brainchild of architect John Eberson. An elaboration on the "plain" picture palace, the atmospheric gave the patron the impression of being outdoors, seated under the sky. The elaborate architectural and trompe l'oeil effects typical of the palaces, which might give the impression of a Spanish castle or Hindu temple, or some combination of the two, were now outdone, these wonders compounded by the experience of clouds passing over and stars twinkling above. In Eberson's own words, the auditorium was "a magnificent amphitheatre under a glorious moonlit sky . . . an Italian garden, a Persian court, a Spanish patio, or a mystic Egyptian temple-yard . . . where friendly stars twinkled and wisps of clouds drifted." Eberson's first atmospheric theatre was built in Houston, Texas, in 1923, and the style became immensely popular. Eberson himself turned out innumerable atmospherics and had many imitators as well. The enterprising theatre owner could even buy his own "Brenograph," a projection device that created stars and clouds and other scenic affects, and create atmospheres of his own.

Wolfe feels fortunate that he was able to work with a man like Boyd, who grew up with the industry through its heyday in the twenties and thirties. When he took over the Roxy in 1970, the age of the "twin" theatre had already arrived. By the mid-seventies there were triplexes and quadraplexes, and there is even one complex in Canada now with twenty screens.

Wolfe goes on to talk about taking over the Roxy and his efforts to bring it back to life:

"I wanted to run the Roxy as an old-time theatre, but business was so bad in the beginning that after a couple of weeks I cut it back to a four-day operation, Friday through Monday. And I only kept Monday because the stores were open late. I can remember standing out in front on Monday night and seeing all these people go in and out of the stores but not coming into the theatre. So I gave up on Monday and just ran it on the weekends for about four years. No matter how many people show up, the box office has to stay open the entire time because you don't know if someone is going to walk in fifteen minutes or a half-hour late, or whatever. The policy in the big downtown theatres used to be to turn off the arc lights of the projector, and turn off the sound system, and just run the film through. The theatres usu-

EMPIRE
Watercolor on paper, 1985
14¾ x 10 in. (37.5 x 25.4 cm.)
Collection: Louis K. and Susan Pear Meisel, New York, N. Y.

ally had long lobbies, so if somebody walked up to the box office and bought a ticket the cashier could buzz the projection booth, 'somebody's coming,' and by the time they got to the auditorium everything was on.

"The very first day I had the theatre I painted the front, everything below the marquee, to get rid of that beige and black. I found out right away that the the former owner didn't turn the marquee on because it didn't work. Thirty-eight light bulbs lit out of about five hundred. And only two or three tubes of neon lit. None of the "Roxy's" lit up at all. I did get the chaser unit around the attraction panel working—only a couple of bulbs lit and so I replaced all the rest that first day too. It's amazing how many people came in the first couple of weeks and said they were really glad to see someone had reopened the theatre. They thought it had been closed for a couple of years.

"It took me several years to get the marquee going again. I had to replace all the bulbs and a lot of bulbs had broken off in the sockets. We have a problem in town because this is a cement town, not as much as it used to be but still pretty active. If you look in an old encyclopedia of the twenties or thirties you'll see Northampton listed as the cement capital of the world. There were five or six cement plants here. All the cement for the Panama Canal came from Northampton. As a result we had terrible pollution—cement dust. This very fine cement dust would get into the sockets around the bulbs. Then it would rain and the moisture would get in and the bulbs would be cemented into the socket. Every time you wanted to take a bulb out it would break right off and then you have to use pliers, or whatever, and work on the socket. I had hundreds of bulbs cemented into their sockets to contend with. It still happens a little bit, but not nearly as much.

"One of the projectionists who had worked here for many years brought in an early photograph one day which showed the marquee. Using that, I painted the marquee one summer. Once I started, I realized that if I looked really closely I could still see the design even though it had been painted over. The zigzag design and that kind of candy-cane motif—so I was able to trace it. It was about 1977 that I had it all working and painted to the original colors.

"Just last year I discovered a new photograph of the theatre a few weeks after the original renovation—strangely enough, in the files of the Boyd in Easton, even though the two theatres never had anything to do with one another—and there were only a few small elements of the design painted differently then, like a darker edge around the Roxy lettering, so next time the marquee gets painted I'll incorporate them."

It took about two years before Wolfe broke even at the Roxy, and it wasn't until 1975 that he made a profit. Then he went back to a seven-day operation. In keeping with the theatre's origins as a combined vaudeville/movie operation, he instituted live entertainment, putting on rock shows in conjunction with a local disk jockey. These shows were a fantastic success. They ran films five or six days a week and live shows one or two and the shows brought a lot of new people into the theatre. The theatre got a lot of publicity and became increasingly well known. They still do a live show once in awhile, but basically the Roxy is back to being a movie house—although the way Wolfe puts on a movie is a show in itself.

One of the interesting aspects of the Roxy's success is the audience demographics. Not only are people willing to drive forty or fifty miles, passing many multiscreen theatres along the way, to come to the Roxy, but it isn't just people bent on a nostalgia trip. Young people enjoy the atmosphere and appreciate a true movie-going experience too. As Wolfe puts it: "I have something those new places don't have. I have a theatre—they have a shoe-box cinema. They can show first-run films ahead of me, but they can't offer what I can, the atmosphere of going to the theatre."

THE PAINTINGS AND THE THEATRES

HOLLYWOOD GOES DECO
A NEW STYLE FOR A NEW AGE

MARION WITH THREE CARS
Acrylic on canvas, 1985
48 x 38½ in. (121.9 x 97.8 cm.)
Collection: Dr. and Mrs. Donald J. Mayerson, New York, N. Y.

As we have seen, the history of movie theatres is intertwined with the history of movies themselves and with the efforts and influence of particular individuals, architects and impresarios, who understood intuitively something about the magic this medium possesses. From its flickering infancy at the turn of the century, film quickly grew and developed to become the quintessential art form of our age, providing our fantasies and producing images of ourselves that came to have tremendous power over our conscious and unconscious thoughts and desires. But if movies helped to form our age, they were also formed by it. Scientific, historical, economic, and cultural forces all worked together to foster growth and change. And the environments in which we watched the movies evolved as well, reflecting the changing needs of the new medium and the changing needs of society. Like the Atlanta Loew's and the Northampton Roxy, old theatres were renovated to suit new times and many new theatres were built: the glory days of the small hometown theatre, which Davis Cone evokes so beautifully in his paintings, was at hand.

We had had *palaces, shrines,* and *temples* to the motion picture, but by the time Roxy Rothafel's "Cathedral" opened in 1927 it was already a dinosaur: the time of these monumental extravaganzas was past and the demise was hastened by the cumbersomeness of their scale. They had "elaborated" themselves out of existence with their "more is better" philosophy. But other factors were at work as well. In spite of popular belief to the contrary, the Depression did take its toll on the movie industry. In 1931 weekly film attendance in America dropped from ninety million to sixty million people, and it continued to drop in 1932, hitting rock-bottom in March 1933 at only forty percent of what it had been in January 1931. The coming of sound had staved off the damage for a couple of years after the crash by inspiring a movie-going boom of its own.

In 1927, *The Jazz Singer* brought to film both the incredibly popular singer Al Jolson and the first words heard on film that actually advanced the plot—Jolson exclaiming, "Wait a minute, wait a minute. You ain't heard nothing yet!" The long quest for viable sound in the movies was over (although the use of a sound track on the celluloid was yet to come and the technique still required records timed to play with the film); the craze for "talkies" had begun. Talkies were a great boost for the movie industry. Competition from radio (in spite of Roxy's optimism), mediocre product, and general movie-audience malaise had slowed the growth of business in the mid-twenties. But though talkies filled theatres in the last years of the decade, they were one more nail in the coffin of the picture palaces. The new sound movies proved incredibly compelling on their own; they did not require orchestras to accompany them, and stage shows even more elaborate than Roxy's extravaganzas could be put on film and shown anywhere. Large stages, orchestra pits, and other vestiges of the vaudeville era became obsolete.

For the very reasons the talkies helped to end the reign of the picture palaces, they made possible the glory of the small-town theatre where now anyone could partake of the magic. As an announcement in *Publix Opinion*, the weekly paper for the theatre chain's managers, put it: "Sound shows now put every Publix theatre in the deluxe class. . . . from this day forward every Publix theatre is a deluxe theatre." It no longer mattered if you were in Gainesville, Georgia, watching the movie at the Show theatre, or at the Time in Mattoon, Illinois, or at any of the other small theatres across the country; the viewing and listening experience you had would be the same as that of the patrons in the biggest theatre on Broadway. From now on, when it came to the movie-going experience, everybody would sit in first class.

If the new sound was drawing people into the theatres, so was a new look. In 1928, Cedric Gibbons designed the first film with a modernistic all-deco decor, *Our Dancing Daughters*. This was quickly followed by Van Nest Polglase's

The Magnificent Flirt. Soon other designers like Cecil B. De Mille embraced the style, creating marvelously luxurious modern sets that the studios promoted heavily, advertising such enticements as "smart society, gorgeous gowns" and "modernistic settings." There were deco homes and apartments, deco baths, deco offices, and deco hotels. Thanks to talkies, nightclubs became a popular setting, providing films with an occasion for music and dance and a chance to inject some high-style elegance. Universal's first all-talkie, *Broadway,* was based on the hit play of the 1926-27 stage season and featured an incredibly lavish art deco cabaret. The new style was a bonanza for Hollywood, ever on the lookout for novelty, drawing patrons who were dying to see what this new "modernistic" trend was all about. And once they saw it, they wanted more.

No style is more identified with the glamour of Hollywood than art deco. Its sleek lines and gleaming curves bespeak an unutterable luxury. It was the style of luxury liners, soaring skyscrapers, and fantastic nightclubs, and of the Hollywood sets that glorified them and gave most of us our image of what they looked like. As Howard Mandelbaum and Eric Myers state in their marvelous treatise *Screen Deco:* "If movies promised life, liberty, and the pursuit of riches, then Art Deco provided the perfect setting." Hollywood didn't invent art deco, but it embraced it with such enthusiasm that it created a substyle all its own, at once more flamboyant, more sleek, more stark, more luxurious—and impossibly chic.

But what actually is art deco? It is one of those terms that is at once so general that to many people it covers anything designed during the thirties, and so specific that to others the only true art deco is the French style of the twenties, which evolved out of the *Exposition Internationale des Arts Décoratifs et Industriels Modernes* held in Paris in 1925.

Though the French show made a tremendous impression in Europe and America, other influences came into play al-

PARK (opposite)
Acrylic on canvas, 1980
43½ x 47 in. (110.5 x 119.4 cm.)
Collection: Mr. and Mrs. Robert Saligman,
Gladwyne, Pa.

PITMAN
Acrylic on canvas, 1983
54 x 39¾ in. (137.2 x 101 cm.)
Private Collection, Fresno, Calif.

most immediately. Displaying a thrust toward a rectilinear, geometric style, French art deco nevertheless tended to be ornate, with an emphasis on rich woods, elaborate inlays, and other decorative elements; and it was highly influenced by the curving lines and floral themes of art nouveau, which preceded it. By the end of the twenties, however, the influence of cubism, of the International style, and of the "machine age" temper of the times had won out and a more austere style held sway. At the time, the French style was called art moderne, and its adaptations were referred to as "the modernistic" or "the moderne": the term art deco was not coined until 1966, at the time of the retrospective of the Paris show.

These names were apt because it was during the late twenties and thirties, with the help of these designs and the inventions that spawned them, that the modern world truly became modern. In America, industrial designers (a new concept in itself) such as Raymond Loewy and Walter Darwin Teague had enormous impact with work that responded to the imperatives of the new age. It was an age of rapid change in society and also an age of unprecedented optimism about progress. At the heart of their work was an embracing of the future, of technology, of the new, fast-moving pace of the modern world. Streamline became the buzzword and the impetus behind the new, simple, dynamic designs. Industrial materials were prized for their sleek, hard surfaces and light-refracting capabilities, for their mass-producibility, and simply because they *were* industrial. Aluminum, stainless steel, and glass block found their way into private homes and, of course, onto Hollywood sets. The identification of Hollywood chic with these new materials was so great, in fact, that a magazine ad for glass block featured Shirley Temple beside a glass block playhouse, trowel in hand, with the implication that it was both fit for a star and so easy to use "even a child can do it."

It is this streamline deco, or American deco, as it has been called, that most of us think of when we say art deco and that is most identified with Hollywood, although the two impulses—the French toward decoration, the American toward streamlined simplification—continued to coexist and find expression in the design of the period.

It is one of those historical anomalies that while this period is identified with the extreme luxuriousness of Hollywood deco, it is also the period of the Great Depression. As the Depression deepened, the incorporation of industrial materials and simplified, undecorated shapes prevailed, showing the increasingly democratic outlook of those American designers who wanted to create practical, good, clean designs that would be available to everyone and would improve the quality of modern life. Hollywood deco tended to ignore the democratic underpinnings of this new direction and concentrated on its rich surfaces. Film is, after all, a visual medium, and all that chrome and aluminum and white satin played well on the silver screen, bringing to the fantasy a new luminosity. Far from prompting an end to all this indulgence, the Depression fueled the public's desire for just such glittery "wish-fulfillment" interludes, which offered escape from the harsh reality of the everyday world and, in their own way, fostered an image of a brighter future.

The sleek, sometimes stark, surfaces and airy, open spaces of the new Hollywood sets were liberating and titillating. They represented the throwing off of the cloak of the old and the embracing of the new. And the new was often seen as risqué. It was always the divorced woman or mistress who lived in the sleek white apartment. while the wife or girl next door retained a cozy, traditional decor. As an actual style of interior design, art deco never did find its way into very many homes, but in the Hollywood sets of the late twenties and thirties (and in the much publicized homes of the stars) it found its way into our imaginations, and with Hollywood's help, came to define an era.

Although the age of the picture palaces was over, a few were still being built, and the great deco palaces were the

REGENT
Acrylic on canvas, 1985
42½ x 51½ in. (108 x 130.8 cm.)
Collection: Amy Odessa Karp, New York, N. Y.

TIME (opposite)
Acrylic on canvas, 1983
59¼ x 45¾ in. (150.5 x 116.2 cm.)
Speyer Family Collection, New York, N. Y.

swan song of this genre. The fabulous Radio City Music Hall, which opened in New York City during the throes of the movie-going decline of 1932, was the last. It has managed to survive threats of closure and demolition, and remains the only picture palace operating today with live shows more or less under its original format. Radio City was Roxy Rothafel's swan song as well. He had left his own theatre to manage this new extravagant usurper, but he was old and ill, and his was no longer the spirit of the age. He left shortly after Radio City opened, but his high-kicking "Roxyettes" remain, although they were renamed the Rockettes in a legal dispute with the Roxy theatre over a name that, ironically, he could no longer call his own.

It might seem a huge leap from the luxury of these sleek monoliths and of the new Hollywood sets to the small-town neighborhood theatres chronicled in Davis Cone's paintings, which perhaps boast nothing more than a few curves and strategically placed bands to announce their deco origins. But these theatres carried the magic and the message of deco with them into the hinterlands. The concept of what was glamorous had changed from the opulence of the mythical past to the sleekness of the new moderne. The presence of even a few signature visual and architectural devices that evoked the new modern style announced *Hollywood* and conjured dreams of all the luxury and excitement that entailed. People might not want to welcome these shapes into their homes, but they were delighted to watch their favorite stars frolicking in modern sets in theatres that brought all the glamour a little closer to home. And as Cone's paintings reveal, for many of these theatres the secret of their appeal lies in the very modesty of their glamour.

As Cone said, describing the theatre in MARTIN: TAL-LEDEGA (p. 31): "You have all these typical Southern buildings of the nineteen-twenties and thirties and then you see the theatre front and the marquee coming out with its black Vitrolite tile and Aztec design and it's so out of place. It was like they said, okay, this is Hollywood so we'll suspend our judgment, the confines of what should be, and we'll let it be flash, we'll let it be gaudy. It's a little bit of Hollywood in Talledega, Alabama.''

The sleek simplicity of the new style was a boon to the theatre companies, for while deco was associated with luxury, it was a luxurious look much less expensive to achieve than the extravagant fantasies of the picture palaces that preceded it, with their layer upon layer of ornamentation. It didn't take long to figure out that some high-style chrome, aluminum, Vitrolite tile, and glass block could wow the patrons for much less money.

The Park, set off to perfection in Cone's evocative portrayal (PARK, p. 54), has a classically perfect deco marquee. The white tiles of the V-shaped marquee are surrounded by a simple red neon band that is gently arched along the top. Large blue neon channel letters are silhouetted against the building, and six wavy white neon lines add side interest at the edge of the marquee and accent the prominent geometric center post. Also outlined in red neon, and accented with a large white neon "P," this is its most striking feature.

Like the designs on the Martin in Talledega, the stylized geometric motif on the Park shows the influence of Indian—in this case Mayan—themes. This was the great age of international travel, and deco incorporated not only the streamline look of modern means of transportation—the train, the plane, and the luxury liner—but also the influence of ancient cultures. Mayan, Aztec, African, and Egyptian motifs were all stylized and assimilated into the deco vernacular. After Sid Grauman opened his Chinese theatre in Hollywood in 1927, this oriental influence was embraced by other designers. Stylized and hybridized as these elements became, it is sometimes difficult to tell exactly which cultural legacy is intended. The large round central medallions of the theatre in HAPPY HOUR (p. 67) with its pagoda-style logo made from the H H T of the name are distinctly Chinese and might

WILKES (opposite)
Acrylic on canvas, 1981
45 x 45 in. (114.3 x 114.3 cm.)
Collection: Richard Brown Baker, New York, N. Y.

WINK
Acrylic on canvas, 1981
42½ x 47½ in. (107.9 x 120.6 cm.)
Collection: Dr. Barry Paley, Rye Brook, N. Y.

well have been intended to remind patrons of the huge gong outside of Grauman's theatre. But what of the discreet geometric corner motifs of the Knox, or the designs flanking the lettering atop the marquee of the Sam Eric—are they Chinese, or Aztec, or Mayan?

The two most dominant visual themes of the period and of the marquees are, however, the curve and the decorative band, and they both derive from the streamline impulse. As Martin Greif states in his study of the design of the 30s, *Depression Modern,* the curve grew out of concern with aerodynamics and was expressive of the tension, vigor, and energy of the new age. While today we think of streamline as a verb or adjective, there was an actual design motif in the 1930s called "the streamline," a line with a "sharp parabolic curve at the end," which, despite the practical origins of the concept, was applied to all kinds of things like housewares and furnishings that never move and have no need to be adapted to the flow of air currents. As Greif observes, this line, reduced to a few curving bands, appeared on almost everything designed during the thirties and became a shorthand for modernity.

These are the bands that show up in one form or another on the theatres in MARTIN: TALLEDEGA (p. 31), THOMPSON (p. 66), WINK (p. 63), PITMAN (p. 55), AVON (p. 14), MARIANNE (p. 30), and on practically every theatre in Cone's paintings and of the period. The round marquees in MILLER (p. 99) and SAM ERIC (p. 71) reflect the same aerodynamic impulse. But it is GREENSBORO THEATRE (p. 90) that, in spite of the sadly decrepit state the theatre had reached by the time Cone painted it, presents the best example of streamline design. Although essentially a "V" shape, the marquee stretches the entire length of the theatre's façade. Neon bands begin with a curve at the edge of the building, sweep around the "V," and move on to a final curve at the far corner. The sense of flowing motion is enhanced by two additional short bands at each curve, while the faceted aluminum panels in the side sections, designed to reflect and enhance the neon glow, reinforce the design's industrial derivation. Accentuated by Cone's strong, offset composition, the curved nose of the marquee thrusts forward like the nose of one of Raymond Loewy's streamlined locomotives. In the dark night of a small town, all its neon stripes aglow, it must have seemed the very embodiment of the future.

The Thompson Theatre sports a similarly shaped marquee, but it is only one part of a complex design. Streamline bands are used here as well, not only on the projecting nose of the marquee but also with a particularly jazzy flourish on the crown of the vertical name sign. This theatre is a charming hybrid, incorporating in a style that can only be called small-town kitsch several seemingly disparate elements of the deco period.

This was the age of the skyscraper boom, and skyscraper style added its own influence to the deco mix, particularly in the form of the stepback motif or design on vertical surfaces. The result of zoning ordinances in Manhattan, this architectural motif gained by association the aura of glamour, wealth, and progress characterized by such buildings as the Chrysler and the Empire State, although in some designs it is difficult to tell whether a skyscraper or reference to Mayan or Aztec pyramids is intended.

The Thompson is a case in point. The vertical element is a skyscraper reference reinforced by the tricolored stucco bands in the stepdown style on either side, as well as by the pattern on the front of the building, and by the glass block windows that flank it. But the stucco elements could certainly be seen as Mayan as well. The unique set of streamline bands that top the vertical sign form a narrow curve in front, sweeping back and down into a fan shape. The result looks something like a cross between an Indian headdress and the front of a speeding train. This then is topped with what appears to be another skyscraper reference, a small spire supporting a metal disk like a Chinese hat or half a cym-

THOMPSON (opposite)
Acrylic on canvas, 1980
55 x 39 in. (139.7 x 99.1 cm.)
Private Collection, Geneva, Switzerland

HAPPY HOUR
Acrylic on canvas, 1984
29 x 74 in. (73.7 x 188 cm.)
Collection: Birlane Foundation, New Orleans, La.

bal that either is, or is meant to look like, an antenna. Down the front of the vertical sign run a pair of neon zigzags, reinforcing the Indian references. The main marquee, with its simple lines, dignified block letters, and chrome bands, seems almost to belong to a different theatre—until we see the waterfall neon band and neon curlicue that flank the central medallion.

The overall effect, particularly with the colored stucco, might be called Southwestern/skyscraper. This combination seems especially odd for a theatre in Georgia. However, the stepback design was often used as a catch-all for the conflicting impulses between big-city glamour and primitive simplicity. And it is precisely this kind of confusion, this naïve desire to embrace every current design motif at once, that gives such small-town pastiches their quirky charm.

An even more eccentric interpretation of skyscraper motif is found in WINK (p. 63), with its three-tiered neon wedding cake atop another "V" marquee. The simple but unique white cylinder, which rises from the center, appears to be in competition with the dome of the public building across the way, on which the whole apparatus seems to be modeled—an odd case of a theatre designer attempting a glittery salute to the classical affectations of the surrounding architecture. Beneath the "V" marquee of the Wink sits a sleek, curved ticket booth in a classic streamline style that seems as out of context with the whimsical structure above it as the entire structure does with the town.

Various elements of these theatres could be ordered from the annual *Theatre Catalog,* a publication that combined articles on theatre design, drawings, and descriptions of new theatres with advertisements from suppliers and designers. Doors, ticket booths, seats, lobby display panels, and letters could all be chosen from readymade designs. And while some designers or theatre owners were content to repeat the standard pattern of the day—"V" marquee with neon block letters with or without some neon streamline bands rounding the nose—others were inspired to greater and lesser flights of fancy.

Designers also had available to them Philip Dilemme's two volume *Luminous Advertising Sketches,* a popular handbook of inventive neon designs that included instructions on the practice of design, the building and painting of electric signs, and the bending of "luminous tubing," as well as hints on presenting and selling designs and design services. There are many prototypical art deco marquees included.

Rudi Stern, in his introduction to the recent reissue of Dilemme's book, comments on the "fluid exuberance of American Deco signage." The small-town theatre marquee afforded an opportunity for experimentation and for individual flights of fantasy or whimsy; neon as a design element offered unlimited potential for expression because of its ability to be bent or curved to follow any shape. The designer of the theatre in BAD AXE (p. 2), inspired by the name of the town, was able to create somewhat crude, endearingly naïve, and descriptive neon axes, while the sign for the Stardust Drive-In employs a more typical star motif. The marquee in VARIETY PHOTOPLAYS (p. 22), demonstrates a marvelously fluid and delicate use of neon tubing in the outline of its intricate patterning, which seems to demonstrate with its curves, angles, and curlicues a combined French/Mayan influence.

The vertical marquee or name sign was a standard embellishment for those who wanted something more than the basic overhanging marquee, and it, too, was open to a great variety of interpretation. The spire in WILKES (p. 62) reaches higher than the roofs of the modest buildings around it, piercing the sky with a stylized feather point that clearly owes more to the Mayan or Indian than skyscraper influence, while the Pitman offers a simpler, more classic deco pylon attached to the building façade and accented by horizontal neon bands. The theatre in TIME (p. 59) was "keeping up with times" with its name and large central clock, which together

CINEMA
Acrylic on canvas, 1988
15½ x 29 in. (39.4 x 73.7 cm.)
Collection: Jesse Nevada Karp, New York, N. Y.

SAM ERIC (opposite)
Acrylic on canvas, 1982
30¾ x 40½ in. (78.1 x 102.9 cm.)
Collection: Mr. and Mrs. Martin Z. Margulies, Miami, Fla.

conjure images of Times Square and its cornerstone, the *New York Times* building. Its V-shaped glass block tower is certainly the epitome of skyscraper éclat. In another vein, the vertical motif on the marquee in MARIANNE (p. 30), a pale yellow cylinder topped with three orange circular bands, resembles the smokestack of a steamship, and the prowlike projection right below it reinforces this reference, unusual for a Kentucky movie house. On the Marion, in Ocala, Florida, (MARION WITH THREE CARS, p. 50), this ocean liner theme is played out in a more conservative fashion. With its pale stucco façade, porthole windows, louver-like grilles, and stylized smokestack name tower, it is a classic example of tropical deco.

During the period from 1933 to 1938 the number of movie theatres in America increased from 13,416 to 16,251. At the same time, the advent of sound encouraged the closing or remodeling of many of the larger, older theatres so the actual number of theatres designed or redesigned in the new style was much greater. By 1948 almost four thousand more theatres had been built in what had become a deco theatre vernacular, an offshoot of Hollywood deco and a subgenre all its own. This remained the prevailing style for theatre building throughout the forties and into the fifties. It wasn't until the advent of the mall cinema in the early sixties that a distinctly new style evolved, a style that with its boxy shapes and impersonal signs makes the innocent charm and whimsical individuality of the deco theatres all the more precious and appealing.

THE PAINTINGS AND THE THEATRES

UNDER THE STARS
THE RISE AND FALL OF
THE DRIVE-IN

It was probably inevitable that at some point America's love affair with the auto and its love affair with movies would combine to form that bizarre hybrid, the drive-in theatre. What is surprising is that it happened as early as it did.

The earliest prototype for the drive-in is the mobile picture show, which sprouted at the same time as the early nickelodeons. Like a traveling fair or circus, the mobile picture exhibitor would move from town to town, setting up the screen in a public square or other appropriate place and often projecting the movie from the roof of a van. But this form of movie exhibiting never gained any substantial popularity in this country, although it was fairly popular in England, because local merchants in towns all over America were quick to see the profit to be made in converting available buildings and storefronts for the viewing of·moving pictures. And while the result of these mobile picture shows was an outdoor movie theatre, its limitations were severe since it was the theatre that was mobile rather than the patron.

The first actual drive-in theatre, the Camden, on Wilson Boulevard in Camden, New Jersey, was built in 1933, when the movie industry was just beginning to recover from the Depression and the nation was still a long way from prosperity. The brainchild of Richard Milton Hollingshead, Jr., it was advertised as the "world's first automobile motion picture theatre. . . . sit in your car, see and hear movies." There were accommodations for four hundred cars and, failing to foresee the difficulty those in the back seat would have seeing over the heads of those in front, Hollingshead had optimistically expected to have four patrons per car. Individual post speakers had not yet been developed, so the sound also presented something of a problem. It was claimed that the volume was acceptable up to five hundred feet, but windows had to be kept open. Sitting through the feature on a hot, mosquito-filled evening must have been a trial, but a chilly evening would not have been very comfortable either.

But then the comfort afforded by going to the drive-in

has always been a rather peculiar variety. The speakers, even when they had them, produced a thin squawk and required enough of an opening on the top of the window to induce a brisk sale in mosquito coils. (The broadcasting of the soundtrack directly through the car radio is a more recent innovation.) In between the films—long after they were given up at the regular theatres, double features remained the norm at the drive-in—you had to endure a ten- or fifteen-minute intermission. The exhortations to run to the snack bar to purchase the luridly purple hamburgers and green french fries flashed on the screen were punctuated by a cartoon clock that appeared with the announcer's message—only ten, or seven, or five more minutes to visit the snack bar. You held out as long as you could, only to succumb in bored desperation right before the next feature was ready to begin. But then, it hardly mattered. The view was actually better outside the car than in.

Still, the Camden must have been something of a success since others followed in its wake, although they did not exactly spring up like mushrooms. By the end of World War II there were still only a hundred drive-ins; but their slow proliferation was partly due to factors caused by the war itself. The scarcity of both building supplies and labor halted most domestic construction, and gas rationing was an anathema to the drive-in concept.

The immediate postwar period, however, was a boon to this fledging enterprise. The baby boom, the auto boom, and suburban migration all came at once. By 1948 there were 820 drive-ins in America. By 1954 there were 3,000 more. In 1958 the number of drive-ins peaked at 4063. The last figure is particularly interesting, because by this time TV was taking a severe toll on movie theatre attendance; the proliferation of the drive-ins actually boosted movie company revenues for a short time.

But from the start, exhibitors were aware of certain built-in problems. The 1945 *Theatre Catalog* contained an illustrated

ATHENS DRIVE-IN
Acrylic on masonite, 1977
34¼ x 24 in. (87 x 61 cm.)
Collection: Evelyn Konrad, New York, N. Y.

article on a proposed new "Drive Over and Drop In" theatre that housed the screen on the outside wall of a large multi-use building. This concept included restaurants, nightclubs, and stores in the building, as well as ice skating on the parking lot in winter. The problem for the drive-in operator was clear—a drive-in required a lot of land but could only be used part of the year in most areas and only at night. And unlike the regular theatre, it could really only accommodate one show. Another article in the same issue addresses this last problem with a design for a "standee area" where cars could line up to wait for a second show, but this was an exhibitor's pipe dream. There is nothing in the romance of the auto that includes anything so suggestive of a traffic jam.

Parking, then again, is something else. If young marrieds with children found the drive-in solved the hassle and expense of a babysitter, teenagers found it supplied privacy of at least a semi-respectable variety. It was not long before the drive-in produced a lore of its own along with an almost inexhaustible supply of nostalgia. For a new generation of suburban and rural teenagers it took the place of the movie-house balcony.

In a way, the very things that caused the drive-in's rise also contained the seeds of its downfall. You didn't have to leave your car, which offered the patron the height of convenience, but cars take up a lot of room per patron. Its appeal to young couples with children was partially convenience but also economic—it was a cheap way to spend an evening. You didn't have to pay a babysitter, and to encourage this part of the audience, children were let in free. Their role as a teen-age passion pit gave drive-ins a somewhat dubious reputation from the start and, when you add to this the one show per evening limitation, it was difficult to get the distributors to give them first-run movies. Of course, none of these things are drawbacks to real drive-in aficionados, who love it all, including the "B" movies.

For many people, being in their car is the next best thing

to being home. In your own car you can relax, take off your shoes, put your feet up, have a beer, and the kids, if you have them, can come in their pajamas and go to sleep in the back seat. It is a kind of sybaritic experience all its own, not like the opulence of the picture palaces but more like slouching on the couch with a bag of Fritos.

Home Box Office and the video cassette recorder, which offer second-run movies at home, have severely cut into this aspect of the drive-in's appeal, however. Even the compact car and bucket seats have done their share in hastening the drive-in's decline. But probably nothing has been more devastating than the rise in real-estate values. An article in *Newsweek* on "The Disappearing Drive-In" noted that a drive-in site outside Parsippany, New Jersey, which cost $10,750 dollars in 1947, was sold to a developer in 1981 for $1.25 million.

It seems clear that the drive-in will soon be disappearing from our landscape, although Texas—home of the world's largest drive-in, the I-45, a six-screener in Houston, and host to the "First World Drive-In Movie Festival and Custom Car Rally" at the North Dallas Gemini—is still a hold out. Perhaps some will be preserved as a kind of sociological landmark.

There is, of course, no actual landmark to preserve, even if someone wished to do so: there is no building to speak of, usually nothing more than a ticket booth, the screen itself, and a cement block snack bar. When a drive-in closes, there is nothing left but a lonely sign and, perhaps, out in a field, the large white rectangle of the screen looming like an enormous tombstone.

The free-standing signboard or marquee of the drive-in is as unique an architectural form as the theatre marquee. The sign is usually both advertisement and entrance marker.Whatever image the drive-in wanted to present to the world, whatever flourishes it was going to use to announce itself, were all in that sign. Davis Cone is fascinated by these architectural oddities stuck so strangely in the landscape, and

he has used the solitary sign configuration to great advantage in both of his drive-in paintings.

The strong structural presence of the sign in ATHENS DRIVE-IN (p. 75), positioned to the far right of the canvas and balanced by the crisscrossing power lines, makes this Cone's most graphic image to date. The red neon letters and white neon bands on the name tower emphasize this strong vertical presence as it rises into the darkening sky. The directional arrow and bright white signboard lead our eye into the painting while their light, reflected back against the base of the tower, not only provides for a beautiful paint passage in the modulating colors but prevents the arrow from becoming too dominant and leading our eye out of the canvas altogether. The dark silhouette of the trees, broken only by the dots of light on the roof of the ticket booth, the tail lights of the receding car and the outline of the pick-up behind it, creates interest and mass at the horizon without detracting from the verticality. The simplicity of this image enforces our awareness of it as an abstract composition, but the same use of compositional elements to achieve both balance and dynamic tension is evident throughout Cone's work.

While the Athens Drive-In afforded Cone a strong graphic presence, the appeal of the Stardust (STARDUST DRIVE-IN, p. 78) is entirely different. Here the freestanding sign rises out of a rural landscape that contrasts and plays up its naïvely flashy period shape. The landscape, with its curving and rutted lane, offered Cone the opportunity to explore more organic shapes than the geometric linear and architectural forms found in most of his Main Street paintings: the rain-slick gravel becomes a vivid pictorial presence in itself.

As these paintings reveal, drive-in signs often display the same design motifs and the same flamboyance as movie marquees, and they seem equally at odds with their surroundings. In both ATHENS DRIVE-IN and STARDUST DRIVE-IN, the natural environment becomes a foil for the vivid, artificial presence of the sign, reinforcing the sense of nostalgia these period anomalies invariably evoke.

STARDUST DRIVE-IN (opposite)
Watercolor on paper, 1986
11 x 10½ in. (27.9 x 26.7 cm.)
Private Collection, New York, N. Y.

THE PAINTINGS AND THE THEATRES

GOODBYE, CRUEL WORLD

THE DECLINE OF

THE HOMETOWN THEATRE

PITMAN (detail)

The 1939 New York World's Fair, whose theme was "the world of tomorrow," featured television among its wonders of the future. Visitors who toured the RCA building saw strange contraptions that looked like large console radios with open mirrored flaps on top that reflected the image from below, and were told that these TVs were the result of RCA's laboratory attempts to add sight to radio—an odd but understandable way of looking at it when one considers that RCA stands for Radio Corporation of America.

Regular TV broadcasts in New York also began in 1939, with the opening of the fair—two hours a week plus coverage of special events. At close to five hundred dollars per set and with hardly anything to watch, few people were buying them. Sound in the movies was only ten years old itself, and few envisioned the changes TV would bring to society or the toll it would take on on this older but still young medium.

The first public television transmission actually took place in a movie theatre, in the form of a broadcast from the RCA offices in Radio City to a console placed in the lobby of the Criterion theatre on Broadway. The Criterion is still owned and operated by B. S. Moss Enterprises, and, according to Charles Moss, current president and grandson of the company's founder, his grandfather was always ahead of his time. Moss started out in vaudeville and went on to own a chain of early picture palaces, including the 116th Street Regent, which Roxy managed when he first came to New York, although the Moss chain took it over at a later date. It isn't hard to imagine how someone who had seen so much change in the entertainment industry would want to share in the excitement of its latest development and might not foresee the ramifications this new wonder would have for his beloved theatres.

The war put any further development or spread of such domestic luxuries on hold, at the same time speeding recovery from the Depression. Hollywood thrust itself into the production of immensely popular patriotic films and was

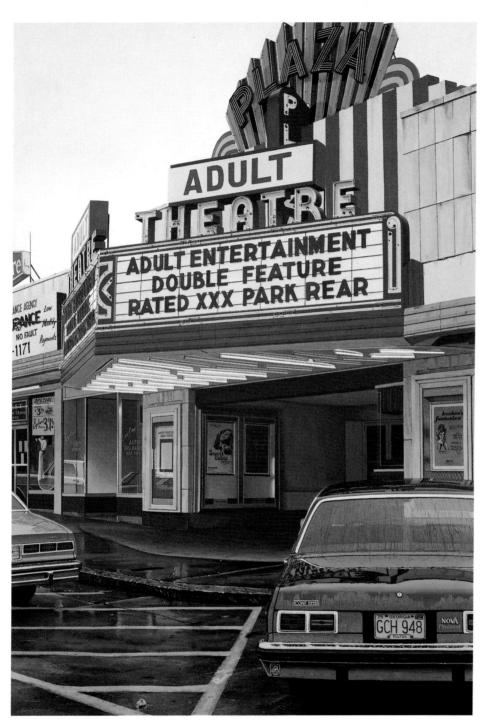

PLAZA
Acrylic on canvas, 1978
62 x 43 in. (157.5 x 109.2 cm.)
Collection: Saul P. Steinberg, New York, N. Y.

SILVER FROLIC (opposite)
Acrylic on canvas, 1980
38 x 48 in. (96.5 x 121.9 cm.)
Collection: Stephen S. Alpert, Boston, Mass.

rewarded with increased attendance that was back to 1930 levels by 1946. With 90 million people once again coming to the movies every week everything seemed rosy, but by then the threat of TV could not be ignored. Statements from those involved with TV took the form of assurances, like the statement made to the *New York Times* by the president of NBC: "Any fears Hollywood may hold that TV will injure motion pictures are ungrounded. . . . nothing will hurt a good picture." Film people, on the other hand, stressed the inadequacy of TV picture quality and size and proposed, in articles with titles like "Motion Picture as An Ally of Television," the establishment of television theatres in which patrons would pay admission to the movie theatre to see large screen television broadcasts. It was a concept that was to have some success with championship boxing matches before the advent of cable TV, but clearly these proposals represented an industry grasping at straws. During the war people had flocked to the movies to see the latest footage from Europe and the Pacific and to hear the official information on the Allied victories and defeats. War bonds were sold at theatres and stars made appearances to help the war effort. But once news became a regular function of television, the appeal of newsreels was gone. Newsreels took days to be developed, edited, and distributed to theatres. TV, as it demonstrated by broadcasting the 1947 Presidential election, could put the news on in a matter of hours.

Movie historians see the televising of this election as the turning point in the nation's acceptance of TV. By 1948, weekly movie admissions had dropped to 70 million. By 1953, they were down to 46 million. In 1958 they reached the lowest ebb in Hollywood history, 39.6 million. Of course, TV alone wasn't responsible, but the currents of the times were on its side. Thousands of GI's had come home, gotten married, bought their first car and their first house and started to raise a family. Television contributed to and benefited from the trend toward staying home that family life fostered. In a

1957 survey it was revealed that eighty-six percent of the people who went to movies also owned a television set, and they were spending more and more nights home watching it.

The period after 1945 also saw a tremendous growth in other forms of recreational activity. Americans turned eagerly to cultural pursuits that were once the province of the elite—art, books, music, and theatre. Interest in sports and outdoor activities increased enormously, as did overseas travel, while staying at home was fueled by the do-it-yourself craze. Movies had to fight harder for the American's leisure time and dollar.

The theatres themselves were up against these trends plus the diminishing desirability of their location. The majority of the new houses were in the suburbs. While this temporarily abetted the growth of the drive-ins, in the end even they succumbed. For the once-glorious Main Street neighborhood theatre, these changes spelled disaster. Between 1948 and 1970 the number of indoor screens dropped fifty percent—to lovers of the old theatres, this is the most devastating statistic of all.

The theatres in Davis Cone's paintings tell their own story. We have already noted the tawdry, low-level fare so many of these theatres are forced to show in their effort to stay alive—*Kung Fu Master, Fist of the White Lotus,* Adult XXX. If there is an ironic poignancy in what many of these grand old theaters are reduced to showing, there is a more muted sadness that pervades the paintings of defunct small-town theatres whose marquees are now empty. Engraved in the stone above the marquee in ORLEANS (p. 115) are the words, "A Monument Devoted to the Best in Music, Photoplay and The Theatrical Arts"—but the marquee is blank. In SHOW (p. 86), the banality and even ugliness of the street, with the yellow and green striped plastic awning jutting out like some cheap imitation of a marquee, underscores the sad hopelessness of the theatre's condition. The plate-glass window, with its

SHOW
Acrylic on canvas, 1979-80
64½ x 41 in. (163.2 x 104.1 cm.)
Courtesy of O. K. Harris Works of Art, New York, N.Y.

PAL (opposite)
Acrylic on canvas, 1978
32½ x 39½ in. (82.5 x 100.3 cm.)
Private Collection, Great Neck, N. Y.

reflection of the opposite side of the street, adds depth and—combined with the view of trees and cars in the distance—creates a compositional and visual interest that seems to relegate the theater irrevocably to its position as "has been."

Other works, such as WILKES (p. 62), with its wide, empty street and deco spire jutting into the expanse of gentle blue sky, and PAL (p. 87), with its pink stone and white marquee looming in the foreground against a sky of majestic clouds and infinite blue, have a more poetic and even elegiac quality. The quietness of the streets and the sense of expansiveness, the openness in the foreground and the sense of infinite depth, work together to create an aura of stillness, of unearthly calm.

The theatre in THOMPSON (p. 66), on the other hand, is portrayed almost straight on, with just enough depth of field for the blatantly blank marquee with its missing tiles to jut out at us with an impressive grandeur. And it *is* grand, with its various art deco textures—the stucco, glass block, neon, and tile, precisely and lovingly evoked—a true monument to Hollywood in its heyday, now defunct, as beat up as the old car parked out front.

In spite of their factuality, these paintings are undeniably romantic, but they are romantic in much the same way that Keats' *Ode on a Grecian Urn* is romantic. The images are clear and clean, the language is spare and unadorned, the mood is evoked by the carefully modulated content. They convey a sense of arrested time. It is a moment on the cusp of change, characterized by that odd combination of sadness and clarity such moments possess.

The mood surrounding the distressed theatres in larger cities is at once more tense and more intense. In AVON (p. 14), the ambience of Providence, Rhode Island is evoked through a highly compressed sense of space and a congested pictorial scene. The cars seem to crowd the sidewalk, the rich textures of the torn posters on the telephone fight the marquee for our attention, and in place of the sense of infinite vista we have the tree, the pole, the marquee, and the roof of the car framing a scene within a scene, increasing the sense of compression. A similar sense of compression occurs in REGENT (p. 58) and EMPIRE (p. 47). In EMPIRE, with its empty marquee in sad disrepair, the compositional elements create a mood of chaos and impending doom. The pole dissecting the picture in the foreground on the right condenses the space even more jarringly with its confrontational presence, while the jauntiness of the façade's blue and white harlequin pattern in the midst of this discouraging scene pierces the air like hollow laughter.

The titles on the marquees in Cone's paintings often have an uncanny relevance. The glare of the sun washing over the corner of the marquee in TIME (p. 59) almost obscures the current attraction, *Staying Alive*—exactly what the theatre seems to be doing. Several of the tiles on the building's fa-çade are chipped, but the neon designs and stud lights seem to be intact. One hopes that it is not just a matter of time before this gem succumbs to the pressures of the modern world.

In Cone's painting MIDWAY (p. 102–103), the marquee bravely announces its name in the gray of a drenching rain. The feature is *The Survivors*. Clearly this theatre is one, but as the only bright spot on this dreary street, we are forced to wonder how and for how long.

And then there is the Knox, never a grand theatre; but in Cone's painting (KNOX p. 35) it has an understated re-finement all the more touching in its current lowly circum-stances. There is a quiet stasis in this painting. Everything looks tired. Weeds grow up around the fading stucco and through the cracked sidewalk; two bent posts mark a dusty driveway; the old Volkswagen parked by the Gulf station looks like it will never move. And yet as the focal point of Cone's painting the theatre seems to regain some of its past glory; like a frail, aging star brought out to be honored one last time, it can

still manage a smile. The theatre is playing *Seems Like Old Times,* and through Cone's fond gaze we can see that some of the old-time magic remains.

The Wink (WINK p. 63) is not as lucky. The theatre is closed, the end of its marquee askew, and in a cruel twist of fate, it is forced to bear the triumphant advertisement for one of its prime competitors, "HBO People Don't Miss Out." The marquee has become a billboard for the owner's new enterprise. In 1971 the Supreme Court cleared the way for pay TV and for the eventual showing of major second-run movies at home. These days movies come out faster and faster on cable and on video cassette, and people feel less and less need to see them in a theatre.

But it is PITMAN (p. 55) that has the most telling marquee of all. Looking at Cone's painting, it is difficult to believe that this glorious, elegant structure is in serious decline. Everything here, however, enhances our awareness of both the beauty of this theatre and the poignancy of its fate. The brilliant sunset against which Cone chose to depict it, is both a metaphor for the theatre's fading glory and a wonderful pictorial device for displaying its remarkable marquee. The darkness of the buildings and street contrasts with the brightly lit marquee and vivid hues of the sky to create an extremely dramatic composition. The light spilling onto the sidewalk from inside the theatre, the white globes of the street lamps glowing against the gold and pink of the sky, the reflections of both lights and sky on the car in the foreground, and the luminous reds and deep mauves on the metal fretwork of the building, are all magical painterly passages that give richness to the scene and enhance our perception of the dominant element.

For at the center of it all is the marquee itself. A few of the neon bands are unlit, the lettering under the "Air Conditioned" sign is dark. And if we look very carefully we can see that the words "Gadsden's Finest" are blanked out. The Pitman may have been "Gadsden's Finest Theatre," but that is a role it will no longer play. Even 99¢ seats didn't save it.

GREENSBORO THEATRE
Acrylic on canvas, 1977
38½ x 56 in. (97.8 x 142.2 cm.)
Collection: Jesse Nevada Karp, New York, N. Y.

The black letters on the bright white tiles spell out its final feature, *Good Bye Cruel World*. The signboard over the entrance, just barely legible in the painting, completes the story. "Garp, At Mall Cinema," it says, announcing the program at the owner's new, more profitable, mall triplex.

Davis Cone tells an interesting story about the Pitman. He had heard about the theatre from a friend and the two of them drove up to Gadsden, Alabama, to photograph it, but when they got there it was deserted. They inquired next door and were told that the Pitman's owner had bought the movie out at the mall. They went to find him and were told that the Pitman had just closed the weekend before. Cone explained that he had driven all the way from Athens, Georgia, and asked if the marquee could possibly be turned on. The man agreed and said his wife would meet them at the theatre to do it. By the time they got back the sun was setting. She went inside and flipped the switch and there it was, all that glorious neon against that incredible sky. When he saw what was showing when it closed, Cone asked her if they had chosen the film deliberately to be the last one to play at the theatre—the irony seemed just too good to be true. It had just been a cheap rental, she said, unaware what the last picture had been until she looked up at the marquee and read it herself.

Like many of the owners of these theatres, she had simply moved on with the business. For although these Main Street theatres are disappearing, the movie industry is doing well. Television is as pervasive as ever, though the networks are finding it harder and harder to hold on to their audience share, but the studios have adjusted to the fact that film attendance will never again reach the highs of the thirties and forties. An increase in the population, however, has meant an increase in potential movie goers. Exhibitors learned through studies done in the early seventies that more people were visiting the cinema than ever before but they were going less often. The multiplex evolved partly as an answer to this problem by offering more choices.

The Roxy flourishes showing second-run movies because the theatre itself is the draw. But this is a unique case. While many of the small-town theatres survive showing these films, a theatre needs first-run product in order to thrive, and these films go to the houses that can offer the greatest return. In many cases the "first-run" houses have to guarantee a certain take, particularly for a blockbuster-type movie. The multiplex cinema helps to insure its owner against loss if a movie does not bring in its guarantee—a fee the theatre owner must still pay the distributor. If the film in Cinema 1 is a dud, the movie in Cinema 2 may do better. The multiplex has numbers on its side. One modern building to heat and maintain, one manager, one projectionist to run the highly automated projectors, one extremely profitable refreshment stand. And several films to attract the patron.

The owners of the Martin theatre chain opened a Cinema I, II, and III outside of Talledega in 1981 and put the original 1936 Martin, with its glorious polychrome, Vitrolite tile façade up for sale. The price, $39,500, was low, but with it went a restriction against using the building as a theatre since the chain did not want the competition for its new triple Martin.

In an even more insidious development, the Sameric theatre chain is suing to block the Philadelphia Historic Commission from designating the Sam Eric an historic landmark. Originally opened as a Boyd theatre on Christmas day in 1928 (by the same company that owned the Boyd in Easton, Pennsylvania, where Richard Wolfe learned the showmanship he later brought to the Roxy), it was nominated, in the commission's words, for its "spectacular art-deco design, which remains almost completely intact both on the interior and exterior."

In Davis Cone's painting we can see, shimmering in the rain, the distinctive curved marquee topped with the green silhouette letters of "Sam Eric" and its red neon stylized Mayan design; down the street the white neon square of the new triplex theatre built to replace it glows brashly. According to an article in the *Philadelphia Inquirer*, the Sameric Corporation has been acquiring properties adjacent to the theatre with the idea of selling the entire property as a major development. Designation by the Historic Commission, the owners claim, would unfairly diminish the value of the property since the new owner could be prevented from tearing the theatre down.

Other theatres, like the Criterion, have themselves been cut up and multiplexed, the only alternative to demolition. If they survive, however, it is usually in a form completely alien to their original existence.

The Happy Hour and the Cameo, on the other hand, survive, as the Roxy did in the seventies, by presenting live performances, and while this represents a valid alternative use for these spaces it also results in some anomalies, like the aggressive rock-and-roll poster in the display case on the front of the pale, dignified stucco façade of the theatre in CAMEO (p. 106).

In looking at his work, one is forced to wonder if Davis Cone would be as interested in painting these theatres if their survival were not so tenuous—or if we would find the imagery as compelling. There is undoubtedly something arresting about their fading glamour; it intrigues us and infuses the paintings with that special sense of nostalgia that characterizes our relationship to small-town America.

THE ARTIST AT WORK

PHILOSOPHY

DAVIS CONE IN HIS STUDIO

As a realist painter in the seventies, Davis Cone was drawn to the work of the first-generation Photo Realists who in the mid-to-late sixties had devised a new kind of American realism, which focused on the commonplace and even banal realities of our postindustrial society. It was emphatically a pre-recorded reality, one that had first been captured by the camera's lens and was then transposed meticulously by the artist on canvas. Through their analytical approach to visual information and their commitment to intense but unemotional observation, they revealed our world to us with a new clarity and extended our notion of the relationship between photography and painting. However, while the work of these artists was influential, Cone soon discovered that the objective stand they took in relation to their subject matter was not fruitful for him.

Photo Realist work was from its inception infused with a documentary ethic that partakes of and comments on the media-inspired information glut that pervades our culture. But this impulse was essentially an impulse toward denotation rather than connotation—toward facts rather than implications. If there was meaning in their choice of imagery it lay in the very ordinariness of the things they chose to paint, and in the fact that it was a subject matter never before embraced by art. Their imagery was deliberately unideal, tarnished by its commonness, and, in the case of the cars, trucks, motorcycles, and fast-food chains that dominated so much of this work, by its associations with blue-collar or mass-culture themes.

The theatres provide Cone with an emotionally compelling and previously untapped subject matter, and the locale of the theatre and the ambience surrounding it are as much a part of the subject matter as the theatre itself. "In looking at each theatre," Cone says, "I try to capture its strange interaction with its surroundings. A writer relies on more than just physical description to portray a character—it is his relationship to the world around him that builds a total portrait.

Likewise, the personality of the theatre is revealed in how it 'sits' in relation to the sidewalk, cars, adjacent stores, signs, etc. As a result, the paintings often become street profiles and the theatre is seen as part of a whole. I feel this information adds to rather than diminishes the importance of the theatre."

Cone's concern with ambience, combined with his interest in Impressionist light, fostered a desire to explore various light and atmospheric situations. The Photo Realists tend to depict their subject matter in a bright, unsparing sunlight that parallels their unsparing objectivity. Cone is unique among this group in making the exploration of different times of day, weather conditions, and light situations a major concern in his work.

Each of the first four theatre paintings explores a different light situation—the spring light of LOEW'S: ATLANTA (p. 27), the bleached summer light of IMPERIAL (p. 19), the twilight of ATHENS DRIVE-IN (p. 75), and the artificial light of MILLER (p. 99). The Miller was one of the Augusta theatres Cone went to as a boy and over the years he had seen it in every type of light. He made it his first night painting because he knew it would lend itself well to this treatment, the bright circular marquee with its tracer lights and red and green neon standing out like a beacon on the almost black street.

While the contrasts in MILLER are extreme, MARTIN (p. 26) was conceived as a study of five subtly different kinds of light—the purplish-blue light of the eastern sky as the last light of day disappears, the eerie green mercury vapor of the street lights, the yellowish tungsten headlights of the cars, the blue-white fluorescent light of the marquee, and the red neon. The lights of the two cars moving in opposite directions converge in front of the marquee in the center of the canvas, highlighting its importance and that of the light itself.

In PARK (p. 54), Cone's most openly sentimental painting, we have a blatantly beautiful image in which the elements of color and form combine to evoke all the wistful, touching charm of a small-town twilight. The pale luminescent blue of the car parked in the foreground leads our eye to the blue neon "Park" and then to the open vista of sky. The muted blues, pinks, and yellows of the setting sun, the glowing neon of the marquee, and the shining metal of the cars, which catch and reflect both the natural and the artificial light, work together to create a rich but subdued tonality. The various elements of the scene are reflected in the Vitrolite tile of the façade, and, in a particularly lovely touch, the fading daylight just picks up the white sleeves of the small figure of a man walking away from us into the evening.

The Plaza (PLAZA, p. 82) was the first theatre Cone painted in the rain. It was a situation that lent itself to a frontal shot. The triangle of yellow parking lines against the wet black pavement echoes the lines created by the neon tubes under the marquee and the blue and yellow band above it; and the diagonal parking afforded an opportunity for the car to become an integral part of the composition. The shape of the windshield repeats the rectangle of the marquee, and the striations of water running down the glass reinforce these structural elements.

Rain, in all its permutations, has provided Cone with the material for several wonderful atmospheric studies. In SAM ERIC (p. 71) the misty night drizzle causes a halo of diffusion around the street light in the upper left corner, which in turn casts an odd greenish glow across the sidewalk, balancing the light from the marquee on the other side of the street. Here, as in ROXY (p. 38) and VARIETY PHOTOPLAYS (p. 22), the jewel-like droplets on the car in the foreground reflect the light and afford Cone the opportunity for some particularly virtuoso painting.

In LANE (p. 15), the mist has cast a sheen on the road and sidewalk but nothing is really wet yet. The drenching downpour in MIDWAY (p. 102–103) gives an entirely different effect. In this painting the ambience of the rain is the strongest element, overriding the lights of the marquee, which just

GREENWICH (opposite)
Acrylic on canvas, 1979
42¾ x 35¾ in. (108.6 x 90.8 cm.)
Collection: Mr. and Mrs. Martin Z. Margulies, Miami, Fla.

MILLER
Acrylic on canvas, 1978
40 x 63 in. (101.6 x 160 cm.)
Collection: Dr. and Mrs. Bruce Maltz, New York, N. Y.

barely make an impression on the overriding grayness. The sense of the rain is accentuated by the spray cast up by the wheels of the moving car, and the overall impression of the deluge is so strong we are tempted to jump out of the way to avoid getting wet.

In GREENWICH (p. 98) it was the image of the marquee projecting over the rain-splattered sidewalk that attracted Cone. The picture was taken on a visit to New York City, when it was all new to him and, as he says, he was still "walking around bug-eyed looking at everything." What interested him was not the theatre's nostalgic content but the exoticism of the visual situation. The red light from the pizza parlor as it spills onto the wet sidewalk is as vibrant as blood against the utter grayness of the street, while the blurred yellow taxi explodes across the center of the canvas, creating an axis of energy from which everything in the painting emanates.

Blurred motion plays an important part in several of these works. While Cone takes great care in planning his paintings, the activity the camera captures is an element that cannot be planned—it can only be appreciated and employed to enhance the realism and excitement of these compositions. In GREENWICH, the taxi streaking by was one of those fortuitous accidents of the photographic process that Cone was not even aware of until the film was developed. The same is true of the streaks of what was actually a fire engine speeding into the frame in SAM ERIC (p. 71). Because he was shooting at a very slow shutter speed, the motion is blurred to such a degree that the vehicle itself is invisible. In CRITERION CENTER (p. 110–111) the frenetic motion of Times Square is implied by the blurred lights of the cars coming toward us as well as by the multitude of people milling on the street and the blazing neon signs against which the theatre marquee must compete for attention.

The use of blur in these works is an unmistakable reference to their photographic origins. For most of the first-generation Photo Realists, this photographic "look" was an important aspect of the work. They were interested in maintaining the awareness of the photo source and in confronting us with the tendency these images have to usurp other, more direct forms of seeing. Cone, on the other hand, is interested in reproducing as far as possible the sense of actually being at the scene he is painting, and except for the evocation of motion, he eschews references to the photograph. There is a balance in his work, however, between the look of directly perceived reality and the look of photographically recorded reality; the pictures are full of that sense of momentary happenstance, of the particular moment caught by the split-second timing of the camera, that is the heart and soul of the snapshot. The light caught raking across a marquee at a certain time of day, a shadow of a power line falling right in the center of a brick arch and across a fender, or a car moving slowly toward us down a desolate street—all offer that specificity of the moment that is so much a part of the Photo Realist aesthetic. But it is in the gestures of the pedestrians caught at odd moments that this snapshot quality is most apparent in Cone's work. The woman with her arm raised in LOEW'S: ATLANTA (p. 27), the cyclist in MARION (p. 116), the seated boy watching the family in COLONIA (p. 107), and the man polishing the metal façade in LANE (p. 15) are intriguing bits of transitory reality that compel us with their artlessness.

While light and atmosphere are a major concern, Cone also has a strong interest in the structural geometry of the paintings and in issues of composition. As the paintings reveal, the placement of the theatres is as variable as the weather. Some theatres lend themselves to a frontal close-up shot, especially if the theatre itself is the most interesting element, but in the majority of cases the street itself is an equally important aspect. In WILKES (p. 62), WINK (p. 63), and MARTIN: TALLEDEGA (p. 31), all painted in the same year, Cone was interested in balancing the composition and

MIDWAY (detail, opposite)

MIDWAY
Acrylic on canvas, 1984
33½ x 49 in. (85.1 x 124.5 cm.)
Collection: Mr. and Mrs. Robert Saligman, Gladwyne, Pa.

making it as symmetrical as possible without having it look symmetrical. In WILKES it is the dark stain in the street that marks the center of the canvas. The result is an unusual composition in which the center is empty. In WINK it is the marquee that is centered. In MARTIN: TALLEDEGA it was the idea of splitting the picture plane in half with the placement of the marquee, the traffic light, and the cars that intrigued him.

EVERETT (p. 23), on the other hand, is almost completely frontal. The theatre and the red brick buildings on either side of it are virtually horizontal to the picture plane, and our awareness of this plane is heightened by the street light at the edge of the canvas in the extreme foreground. In LANE the theatre is on the side and the oncoming car is frontal. Cone has recently become interested in the concept of standing in the middle of the intersection and photographing the scene looking down the street with the cars coming directly at him. This would produce a wide vista encompassing both sides of the street and would also emphasize the deep space by drawing the viewer's eye into the canvas.

While Cone chronicles these scenes, it is an essential rather than an absolute factuality he is after, and he will often modify the photograph, putting things in or taking them out, or altering the color of objects in the scene, if he feels it is necessary to improve the composition. In MARION (p. 116) he added the manhole cover in the foreground to balance the very strong vertical of the telephone pole, theatre sign, and palm tree; and he also based the painting on the information in two separate photographs, adding the section on the far left—which did not appear in the first shot—to give the image a greater sense of expansiveness. In RITZ (p. 34) he took out a white van that was blocking the horizon in the original photograph and destroying the sense of deep space he was after. Sometimes he changes colors to make a better composition. The Volkswagen in WINK (p. 62) was made more orange so the viewer's eye would be led across the painting to the orange stripes above the beauty shop then back down to the gray car, thus creating a kind of inner frame for the marquee.

In his translations of light, however, he remains ardently factual. While this desire to replicate the effects of different types of light grows from the affinity he feels for the concerns of the French Impressionists, the effect of many of his paintings is reminiscent of the works of such Luminist painters as Martin Johnson Heade, Fitz Hugh Lane, John Frederick Kensett, and Sanford Robinson Gifford. These nineteenth-century landscape painters displayed what has been called a particularly American consciousness of light and atmosphere. They are perhaps best known for the astonishing vividness of their sunsets, and it is in relation to a painting such as PITMAN that the correspondence first comes to mind. But the stillness and clarity of light in many of Cone's other paintings also recalls their work, as do the lack of expressive brushwork, the smooth, highly precisionistic quality of the finish, the tendency toward open, expansive compositions, and the emphasis on overall tonal effects.

"The expressive impact of Luminism is dependent on the glassy surface which transforms paint into a substance that shines and emanates," Barbara Novak wrote in a catalog for The National Gallery of Art. She might as well have been writing about the work of Davis Cone, whose paintings shine with an equally radiant twentieth-century light.

THE ARTIST AT WORK

PROCESS

The photographic recording, though factual, is also an interpretation based on the mechanics of the camera lens. While some of the Photo Realists have been interested in exploring the visual idiosyncrasies of the photograph, Cone is concerned with creating an image that reads the way the eye would perceive it. He paints on an extremely smooth surface achieved by stretching the canvas over board and then wet-sanding layer upon layer of gesso. It is not the smoothness of the photographic print he is after, however, but the sense of viewing the scene through the glassy surface of a window.

The camera is an indispensable tool, enabling Cone to capture the myriad details of an ever-changing downtown street, or the color of a particular sunset, or an exact configuration of drifting clouds; but in order to achieve the look he wants; these images must be retranslated out of the photographic idiom. We tend to think of photographic images as absolutely realistic because our eye has become so accustomed to reading them, but the camera actually produces a generalization based on the mechanics of its lens and the chemistry of film. In terms of contrast, for example, the range of detail that can be absorbed in the light and dark areas is limited to a particular speed and lens opening. The camera cannot incorporate the details in extremely bright highlights and at the same time preserve all the details in the deep shadows. As a result, a photograph of a street on a bright day which is set to get the best reading for the middle ground will wash out the sunlit areas and go densely black in the shadows. The pupil of the human eye, however, dilates and contracts continuously, enabling it to make constant adjustments to these differences.

In order to compensate for the camera's tendency to block out detail in the extremely bright and dark areas, Cone first decides the light parameters of the image he wants and then shoots it at several different shutter speeds, underexposing the highlighted areas and overexposing the shadows,

CAMEO
Acrylic on canvas, 1987-88
37 x 45 in. (94 x 114.3 cm.)
Private Collection, Geneva, Switzerland

CAMEO (details)

Comparative photographs. Left image of each set showing underpainting at two weeks. Basic colors and minimal information blocked in. Right image of set at three months, shows refined detail, more subtle value changes and varied textural differentiations.

CRITERION CENTER (painting in progress, overleaf)

Upper left: underpainting at two weeks. Lower left: underpainting at three weeks with only cars not blocked in. Right: completed work all having been repainted—refining and intensifying colors, adding details and texture.

CRITERION CENTER

Acrylic on canvas, 1986-87
39 x 58½ in. (99.1 x 148.6 cm.)
Collection: Mr. and Mrs. Charles B. Moss, Jr., New York, N. Y.

respectively. He also uses a telephoto lens to zoom in and take detailed shots of each area, focusing, for example, on the shadowed doors under the marquee in one shot and the glare on the white marquee in another.

The camera has a limited depth of field and cannot focus on near and distant objects simultaneously. Our eyes, on the other hand, constantly change focus as we look from one object to another, keeping everything in focus as we shift our gaze. Having all areas of the painting in focus, Cone feels, is the best way to approximate this dynamic quality of our vision and results in the most natural look. His method of achieving this is, again, to take several shots of the same scene, focusing on different areas each time. The resulting painting then is a composite, using information from all these different shots. Cone will use as many as one hundred and fifty photographs per painting in this "retranslation" process.

Photographs also generalize when it comes to detail. "Simply because you're working from a piece of film thirty-five millimeters wide, you will never have as much detail when you blow it up as you would see with the human eye," Cone states. "If the texture of the thing you're photographing is smaller than the grain of the film, the film doesn't pick it up, so the surface of the street, for example, has a hint of texture, but it really doesn't have the grittiness you see in real life. Using the information in my detail slides, I can come back into the painting and add more tactile qualities. This enhanced texture also tends to separate the planes of objects and add a heightened sense of depth because photographs tend to condense depth perception as well."

Once he has chosen a theatre to paint and taken the source photograph and all the back-up informational shots he needs, Cone projects the slide on the canvas (or on the paper, in the case of a watercolor) and does a rough, quick drawing. For a large painting, the drawing will usually take about three hours. Then the arduous process of doing the painting begins. Each area requires several thin layers of acrylic, the image becoming both more opaque and more detailed with each layer. While he admires the work of the Impressionists, he aims for an entirely different type of paint surface, one that is completely smooth and free of any indication of the brush strokes or of the texture of the paint. There is no awareness of the artist at work to spoil the illusion he has created, and no signature that would call attention to him. Instead, he hides his name in the lettering of signs and license plates in the painting.

The paintings take three or four months of rigorous discipline to complete, but during this painstaking process there are moments of playfulness when the artist inserts little personal references and jokes into the paintings. His wife's name, Kathy, appears in a vanity plate, their anniversary is on another license plate, a friend's art-supply store was inserted on one of the streets, and the nickname of his art dealer, Ivan Karp, appears as "The Fish" on one of the marquees.

During the painting process the precise information from the slides is augmented by his memories. As he states, "Just remembering the ambience of the scene when you were there sometimes helps you read certain passages in the slide. If it's bleached out, was it because of the film processing or because it was a hot, hazy day? When I was photographing the Time in Mattoon, Illinois, there was a raging sun beating down, in Providence when I took the Avon there was a wet, hazy heat. You remember these things when you're painting and you project them back into the canvas."

While he is painting, he continues to use the slide itself as a reference rather than a photographic print. Viewing the slide backlit on a light box, he feels, gives the most accurate reading of the color, whether it is the neon of a marquee or the sunlight gleaming on a stucco façade, because it is luminescent. A photographic print is seen by reflected light. Working from a backlit slide that is seen through generated light gives a much closer approximation of the experience of painting on location. To an artist who is concerned with light and atmosphere, this is a crucial distinction.

The light he paints under is equally important to him. For many years he painted only under natural light, but this severely limited his painting time. Now he has equipped his studio with full-spectrum light, which is as close as possible to natural daylight. He had a light box built that holds special full-spectrum, Vita-lite fluorescent bulbs, which match the lights illuminating the painting, so that the light source he is seeing the slide through is the same as the light he is painting under. With this method he is able to remain true to the effects of both natural and artificial light captured by the camera.

COLONIA
Watercolor on paper, 1985
10½ x 15 in. (26.7 x 38.1 cm.)
Collection: Richard Brown Baker, New York, N. Y.

ORLEANS (opposite)
Acrylic on canvas, 1979
37 x 25¼ in. (94 x 64.1 cm.)
Collection: New Orleans Museum of Art, Gift of the American Express Co.

THE ARTIST AT WORK

THE FUTURE

MARION
Acrylic on canvas, 1982
47 x 40 in. (119.4 x 101.6 cm.)
Private Collection, Florida

When Davis Cone first began painting the theatres he naturally chose those that were nearby and that he had known from the past. Soon, however, he found himself having to travel further and further afield, either searching out theatres he had heard about or simply driving around taking a hit-or-miss approach. As the radius of his travels grew, the search became increasingly time-consuming, and he found himself devoting more energy to the quest for material than he liked. While he loves the theatres, ultimately they are only the vehicle through which he is pursuing his goals as a painter. He began to worry that eventually he would not have enough time for the actual paintings.

A fortuitous encounter put an end to this fear. As Cone tells it: "With a phone call from photographer Jim Marcus, of Cleveland, Ohio, my involvement with the old movie houses was given new life. On the other end of the line came the passionate voice of a fellow theatre lover who had been traveling for the past ten years all over the country photographing old movie houses. He had heard about me when photographing the Pitman in Gadsden, Alabama. Fortunately, my appearance in Gadsden six months before had sparked the usual inquisitive spectators all wondering why I was taking pictures of the old theatre. Jim's visit brought the same folks out of the adjacent shops who mentioned to him that someone had been there recently doing just what he was doing. They told him I was a painter who showed my work in New York City and his passion for the theatres led him to look me up.

"Jim has taken thousands of slides over the years and soon he started sending me duplicates in the mail, each one meticulously dated with its location marked. Now I could select the theatres that interested me before I set out on a photography trip. There would be no more false leads and wasted effort. It was a godsend."

Cone still goes to photograph each theatre himself, in order to get the particular view and atmosphere he is after,

STATE
Watercolor on paper, 1985-86
14 x 19½ in. (35.6 x 49.5 cm.)
Collection: Dale and Alexandra Zetlin Jones, New York, N. Y.

PLAZA/NIGHT
Acrylic on canvas, 1986
35½ x 56¼ in. (90.2 x 142.9 cm.)
Collection: Michael F. Rakosi, New York, N. Y.

as well as to take the innumerable detail shots he needs. He still worries about how long he can pursue this series because of the alarming rate at which the theatres are being demolished. "While I'm sitting here painting this one, there are probably five more being torn down," he says. "What I really need to do if I want to continue this is to get as many down on film as possible. I'd like to take a trip, to take six weeks off and travel and photograph as many as I can, but it's difficult to take the time away from painting."

The quest for theatres is also a quest for new situations to photograph them in. He hopes to do more paintings of theatres in the snow (there has only been one so far), and to pursue other atmospheric conditions, such as fog, that he has not yet treated. He is also interested in doing more paintings of drive-ins in which he backs away from the solitary sign structure and captures that feeling of a bit of Hollywood set in a lonely, unlikely landscape. His involvement with the effects of thirties and forties neon marquees lit at twilight and at night has led to an interest in the signage of forties and fifties motels, which also beckon in the darkness with their neon and often display a similar charming naïveté and period iconography. He has been photographing them for the past ten years and expects to eventually embark on a new series of paintings based on these images.

As for the theatres themselves, there are some signs of hope. A growing interest in architectural preservation in recent years, combined with an increased appreciation of the role the movie houses have played in our lives, has led to attempts by landmarks commissions to save many of these remnants of our past. Some theatres have gained new life due to these efforts, but sometimes, as we have seen with the Martin, Talledega, it is too late. And as the experience of the Sam Eric shows, economic forces often legislate against these interests.

The imminent loss of a theatre can reawaken an awareness of just how much it means to a community. The State Theatre in Deposit, New York, suffered a disaster in the winter of 1986 when the roof collapsed under a heavy snowfall. Shortly after, a committee, Raise the Roof, was formed to save it. This theatre, with an agate blue Vitrolite glass front and a flamboyant marquee that sports twelve rows of red and blue neon as well as tracer lights along the top and base, was considered the "last word" when it was built in 1937. It remains a sterling example of art deco use of electric light and reflective surface. We can only hope the committee's moneyraising efforts are successful and that the theatre can be preserved and returned to use.

Even changes in the community can sometimes work to a theatre's advantage. The Avon, in Providence, Rhode Island, was distinctly on the seamy side when Cone painted it in 1978, but since then it has become an art theatre, thanks to a new management policy and a renewed interest in "small" and foreign films on the part of the local college audience. The Plaza appears in two of Cone's paintings. When he first painted it, in 1979 (PLAZA, p. 82), it was on its last legs, advertising a triple-X double feature. By 1986 in PLAZA/NIGHT (p. 119), the small shopping center in which it is located had become the focus of a fashionable revitalized neighborhood. A bookstore had replaced the discount insurance broker next to the theatre, a fancy chocolatier was across the parking lot, and in spite of competition from the video store also located in the shopping center, the theatre was advertising a new Sally Field hit and seemed to be thriving.

There is no doubt that time has taken a heavy toll on the movie houses Davis Cone loves; we can only hope that in more and more cases time will now be on their side and that he will continue to paint these marvelous evocations, which record both the time we live in and an era that has passed.

DAVIS CONE: CHRONOLOGY

Biography

1950   Born November 2 in Augusta, Ga.

1968–72   Mercer University, Macon, Ga., B.A. 1972

1972   University of Georgia, Athens, Ga.
Currently resides in New York City

Individual Exhibitions

1979   O.K. Harris Works of Art, New York (Oct 13–Nov.3)

1981   O.K. Harris Works of Art, New York (Jan. 3–24)

1982   O.K. Harris Works of Art, New York (Dec. 11–30)

1983–84   *Davis Cone: Theatre Paintings 1977–1983,* Georgia Museum of Art, Athens, Ga. (Oct 30–Nov. 28, 1983). Hunter Museum of Art, Chattanooga, Tenn. (Jan. 8–Feb. 26, 1984)

1984   O.K. Harris Works of Art, New York (Oct 13–Nov.3)

1988   O.K. Harris Works of Art, New York (Oct. 15–Nov.5)

Group Exhibitions

1977   *Southeastern Artists,* Gertrude Herbert Art Institute, Augusta, Ga. (May 3–13)

1978–79   *Artists in Georgia,* The High Museum of Art, Atlanta, Ga. (Dec. 2, 1978–Jan. 14, 1979)

1979   *Seven Georgia Artists,* The High Museum of Art, Atlanta, Ga. (Sept. 15–Oct. 14)

1979–80   *Southern Realism,* Mississippi Museum of Art, Jackson, Miss. (Sept. 7–Nov. 11, 1979)
University of Mississippi Museum, Oxford (Jan. 21–March 5, 1980)
Roanoke Fine Arts Center, Virginia (May 26–July 9, 1980)
Montgomery Museum of Art, Alabama (July 28–Sept. 17, 1980)
Pensacola Museum of Art, Florida (Oct. 3–Nov. 19, 1980)

INSTALLATION SHOT, OCTOBER 1979,
O. K. HARRIS WORKS OF ART, NEW YORK, N.Y.

1981   *Visions of New York City: American Paintings, Drawings and Prints of the Twentieth Century,* Tokyo Metropolitan Art Museum (March 27–May 24)

1981–83 *Contemporary American Realism Since 1960,* The Pennsylvania Academy of the Fine Arts, Philadelphia (Sept. 18–Dec. 13, 1981)
    Virginia Museum of Fine Arts, Richmond (Feb. 8–April 4, 1982)
    The Oakland Museum, California (May 6–July 25, 1982)
    Gulbenkian Foundation, Lisbon, Portugal (Sept. 10–Oct. 24, 1982)
    Salas de Exposiciones (Recoletos), Madrid, Spain (Nov. 17, 1982–Jan. 8, 1983)
    Kunsthalle, Nuremberg, West Germany (Feb. 11–April 10, 1983)

1984   *Autoscape: The Automobile in the American Landscape,* Whitney Museum of Contemporary Art, Stamford County, Fairfield, Conn. (March 30–May 30)

1985   *Night Lights—19th and 20th Century American Nocturnes,* Taft Museum, Cincinnati, Ohio (May 2–June 30)
    American Realism, The Precise Image, Isetan Museum, Tokyo, Japan (July 25–Aug. 19)
    Daimaru Museum, Osaka, Japan (Oct. 9–28)
    Yokohama Takashimaya, Yokohama, Japan (Nov. 7–12)
    Places Here and Now, Greenville County Museum of Art, Greenville, S.C. (Aug. 13–Sept. 22)

1986   *Nocturnal Imagery,* O.K. Harris Works of Art, New York (Apr. 5–25)

1987   *Nocturnes and Nightmares,* Florida State University Gallery and Museum, Tallahassee. (Mar. 12–Apr. 18)
    Fifty-First National Midyear Exhibition, Butler Institute of American Art, Youngstown, Ohio. (June 28–Aug. 23)
    Urban Visions: The Contemporary Artist and New York, Adelphi University, Garden City, N.Y. (Sept. 20–Nov. 6)

Magazines

New Arts, "For Real," Linn Whittaker, March 1979, pp. 12–13.

Art Voices South, "Southern Realism—A Survey Exhibition," Marda Kaiser Burton, November/December 1979, pp. 25–26.

Contemporary Art/Southeast (vol. 2, no. 6), "Brushed Up Reality," August 1980, pp. 10–11.

Art in America (no. 10), "Southern Realism at the University of Mississippi Museum," Donald B. Kuspit, December 1980, p. 156.

Horizon (Vol. 25, No. 8), "US Arts: Where Business Boosts Arts," Cindy Gnaff Hobson, December 1982, p. 30.

New Arts Review, "Davis Cone Showcases Showplaces," Heidi Elmore, June 1983, pp. 7–8, 15.

Tokyo Journal, "Art: Seeing is Believing," Amaury Saint-Gilles, August 1985, pp. 68–69.

Arts Magazine, "Reviews: Group Show, O.K. Harris," Gregory Galligan, October 1986, p. 127.

Newspapers

Athens (Ga.) Observer, "Photorealism," April 5, 1978, pp. 2B–3B (cover).

Athens (Ga.) Observer, "Close-up: Davis Cone," Merrill Morris, July 8, 1982, p. 4.

Athens (Ga.) Observer, "The Art of Davis Cone," Lee Shearer, October 27, 1983, pp. 1B–2B.

Atlanta Journal-Constitution, "The Select of the Select:

Seven Artists at the High Museum," W. Clyde Burnett, Sept. 2, 1979, pp. 1E–2E

Atlanta Weekly (Atlanta Journal-Constitution), "Grand Illusions," John English, Aug. 3, 1980, pp. 16–19, 25.

Banner/Herald/Daily News (Athens, Ga.), "Cone Exhibit: One-Man Show at Art Museum," Sally Adair, October 29, 1983, p. 5.

Banner/Herald/Daily News, (Athens, Ga.), "Photo Realist Davis Cone: Exhibit of Theatre Paintings Opens at Georgia Museum," Elaine Kalber, October 30, 1983, P. 7H.

Atlanta Journal-Constitution, "Vanishing Movie Theatres Are Vital in Davis Cone's Realist Paintings," Catherine Fox, November 13, 1983, p. 7H.

Chattanooga News—Free Press, "Photo Realist Cone at Hunter Museum," January 8, 1984, p. 4L.

The Chattanooga Times, "Exhibit Opening at Hunter Depicts Vintage Theaters," January 13, 1984.

Cincinnati Post, "Taft exhibition will shed some light on the night," Jerry Stein, April 30, 1985, p. 8B.

Cincinnati Enquirer, "Taft Exhibit 'Night Lights' Illuminative, Highly Seductive," Owen Findsen, May 5, 1985, p. F6.

Lexington (Ky.) Herald-Leader, "Nighttime is star of Cincinnati show," Ann Tower, June 9, 1985, p. D6.

Greenville (S.C.) Piedmont, "Show displays artists' sense of 'place'," Kendra Hamilton, August 20, 1985.

Atlanta Weekly, "Windows of Vision," John W. English, July 20, 1986, pp. 6–15.

Limelight Tallahassee Democrat's Arts and Entertainment Guide, "FSU Gallery Hanging Up Some Nightmarish Visions," Mark Hinson, March 6, 1987.

Florida Flambeau, "Shedding Sharp Light on Murky Evening Shadows," Paul Toomey, March 13, 1987.

Tallahassee Democrat, "Shows Depict Three Views of Art," Betty Rubenstein, March 20, 1987.

New York Newsday, "New York: Grit and Glamor," Karin Lipson, October 2, 1987.

Catalogs

Artists in Georgia, The High Museum of Art, Atlanta, Ga., 1979.

Southern Realism, Mississippi Museum of Art, Jackson, Miss.: John B. Henry III, Tom Dewey, Michael E.Kampen, 1979.

Seven Artists in Georgia, The High Museum of Art, Atlanta, Ga., 1979.

Visions of New York City, Tokyo Metropolitan Art Museum, Tokyo, Japan: Tom Armstrong, 1981.

Contemporary American Realism Since 1960, New York Graphic Society, Boston, Mass.: Frank M. Goodyear, Jr., 1981.

Davis Cone: Theatre Paintings 1977–1983, Georgia Museum of Art, University of Georgia, Athens, Ga.: Linda Chase, 1983.

Autoscape: The Automobile in the American Landscape, Whitney Museum of Contemporary Art, Stamford County, Fairfield, Conn.: Pamela Gruninger Perkins, 1984.

Night Lights, Taft Museum, Cincinnati, Ohio: Heather Hallenberg, 1985.

American Realism, The Precise Image, Isetan Museum, Tokyo, Japan: John Arthur, 1985.

Places Here and Now, Greenville County Museum of Art, Greenville, S.C., 1985.

Nocturnes and Nightmares, Florida State University Gallery and Museum, Tallahassee, Fla.,: Craig Adcock, ed., 1987.

Fifty-First National Midyear Exhibition, Butler Institute of American Art, Youngstown, Ohio, 1987.

BIBLIOGRAPHY

Baxter, John. *Sixty Years of Hollywood.* New York: A. S. Barnes and Co., 1973.

Bergman, Andrew. *We're In The Money! Depression America and Its Films.* New York: New York University Press, 1971.

Bickel, Minnette. "Laments For Loew's Grand," *Atlanta Constitution,* Feb. 10, 1978.

Cerwinski, Laura. *Tropical Deco: The Architecture and Design of Old Miami Beach.* New York: Rizzoli, 1981.

Clarke, Gerald. "Dark Clouds over the Drive-Ins," *Time,* August 8, 1983.

Cohn, Roger. "Chain sues to avert historic status for old movie house," *The Philadelphia Inquirer,* Feb. 11, 1987.

De Give, Henry L., Jr. "When the Grand Was Grand," *The Atlanta Journal and Constitution,* March 5, 1978.

Dilemme, Philip and Rudi Stern. *American Streamline: A Handbook of Neon Advertising Design.* New York: Van Nostrand Reinhold, 1984.

Great American Movie Theaters. Washington, D.C.: The Preservation Press, 1987.

Greif, Martin. *Depression Modern: The Thirties Style in America.* New York: Universe Books, 1975.

Hall, Ben M. *The Best Remaining Seats.* New York: Clarkson N. Potter, 1961.

Hampton, Benjamin B. *History of the American Film Industry: From its Beginnings to 1931.* New York: Dover, 1970.

Historic Preservation. "Martin Theatre, Talladega, Ala." Washington, D.C.: The National Trust, May/June, 1981.

Jowett, Garth. *Film: The Democratic Art.* Boston: Little Brown, 1976.

Langley, Lynn. The Disappearing Drive-In, *Newsweek,* August 9, 1982.

Mandelbaum, Howard, and Eric Myers. *Screen Deco: A Celebration of High Style in Hollywood.* New York: St. Martin's Press, 1985.

McCall, John Clark, Jr. "The Grand," *Console Magazine.* Pasadena, Cal., 1973.

McClinton, Katherine Morrison. *Art Deco: A Guide for Collectors.* New York: Clarkson N. Potter, 1972.

Naylor, David. *American Picture Palaces: The Architecture of Fantasy.* New York: Van Nostrand Reinhold, 1981.

The New York Times: New York World's Fair Section, March 5, 1939.

1941 & 1945 Theatre Catalog. Philadelphia: Emanuel Publications, 1942 & 1946.

Novak, Barbara. "On Defining Luminism," *American Light: the luminist movement".* John Wilmerding, ed. Washington, D.C.: National Gallery of Art, 1980.

Robinson, Cervin and Rosemarie Bletter. *Skyscraper Style.* New York: Oxford University Press, 1976.

Schlosberg, Suzanne. "The Avon Cinema: Perfecting an Image," *Brown* (University) *Daily Herald,* Nov. 11, 1986.

Sharp, Dennis. *The Picture Palace.* New York: Praeger, 1969.

Thompson, Toby. "The Twilight of the Drive-In," *American Film,* July/August, 1983.

Valerio, Joseph M. *Movie Palaces: Renaissance and Reuse.* New York: Educational Facilities Laboratories Division, Academy for Educational Development, 1982.

Wasko, Janet. *Movies and Money.* Norwood, N.J.: Abelex Publishing Corp., 1982.

Wurts, Richard. *The New York World's Fair: 1939/40.* New York: Dover, 1977.